VOICES OF THE PARIS COMMUNE

Revolutionary Pocketbooks

VOICES OF THE PARIS COMMUNE

**Edited and translated by
Mitchell Abidor**

Voices of the Paris Commune
Edited and translated by Mitchell Abidor

ISBN: 978-1-62963-100-4
Library of Congress Control Number: 2015930871

Cover by John Yates/Stealworks
Layout by Jonathan Rowland based on work by briandesign

10 9 8 7 6 5 4 3 2 1

PM Press
PO Box 23912
Oakland, CA 94623
www.pmpress.org

Printed in the USA by the Employee Owners of Thomson-Shore in
Dexter, Michigan. www.thomsonshore.com

■ CONTENTS

■ INTRODUCTION

The Paris Commune of 1871 has been a blank screen upon which schools of radical thought have sought to project their interpretation. The Bolsheviks celebrated its fiftieth anniversary in 1921 by claiming that they were the fulfillment of its promise, and it is said that on the sixty-fourth day of the Soviet government's existence they celebrated their surviving longer than the Commune. Anarchists, too, consider it theirs, an example of working people spontaneously taking power and determining their own fate. Often lost in these appropriations of the event is what the Commune and the Communards had to say, what they fought for, what they implemented, and what they believed. The Commune has been interpreted for over 170 years; the goal of this volume is to allow those who knew the Commune best—those who fought for it, to explain and interpret it for themselves.

Karl Marx's *The Civil War in France,* perhaps the earliest interpretations of the *Commune,* is also the best-known work on the Commune. Despite Marx's support, however, the Commune was not a Marxist-inspired or led revolution. The International Working Men's Association had members who sat on the Commune, but this group, which came to be known as the minority, represented not Marxism but rather a number of trends within the French left of the time. It was largely Proudhonian and strongly republican, and would famously take a strong position against dictatorship and censorship, even threatening to refuse to attend sittings of the Commune when a Committee of Public Safety was to be implemented in its dying days. The bitterness of the debate on this subject can be clearly seen in the transcript from the Commune's *Journal Officiel.* Among the most outspoken opponents of any kind of censorship was Jules Vallès,[1] a member of the International and the Commune, and the editor of the Communard newspaper *Le Cri du Peuple*. The selection of articles from his newspaper included here lends a poetic tinge to the daily life and struggles of the Parisian working class, a portrait he would later expand on in his novel on the Commune, *The Insurrectionist*. The Commune was also not anarchist, as the anarchist movement was all but nonexistent in France at the time and could do little to guide the revolution. Further, the Commune was an elected body, a government, with factions, the germs of a bureaucracy, laws, and an army, thus fallings short of an anarchist model of self-organization.[2] Daniel Guérin would write of the Commune that it was not libertarian, "but to a certain extent "Jacobin."

As many of the voices in this anthology stress, the Commune was a product of a particular place and time—a patriotic and uncompromisingly republican working-class outburst, set off by the French defeat at the hands of the Prussians, the rigors of the siege Paris suffered under, the insult of the Prussian entry into the city, and the onerous indemnities that had to be paid to the victors. Though the Commune was born without ideological parents, it did have a tutelary figure: the tireless conspirator, Louis-Auguste Blanqui. In fact, the Commune itself was preceded by two failed Blanquist uprisings, in October 1870 and January 1871, the first of which had a distinctly patriotic tone, occurring when it was learned that the ruling Government of National Defense was preparing to negotiate with the besieging Prussians. Blanqui himself was held in prison throughout the

1. Vallès, Jules (1832–1885)—Revolutionary journalist and writer. Member of the Commune for the eleventh arrondissement. His *Le Cri du Peuple* was the most successful of Communard newspapers. Sentenced to death in absentia. His novel *Le Révolté* tells of his experiences during the period. Sixty thousand people accompanied his coffin to Père Lachaise Cemetery.
2. France's most celebrated anarchist, Louise Michel, was an active participant in defense of the Commune and later sentenced to deportation in New Caledonia for her actions, but since women were not eligible for election to the Commune, she was simply a rank-and-file fighter. The experience of the Commune helped her along the path to anarchism, but she only became an anarchist during her exile.

life of the Commune by the Versailles forces as a result of the January 1871 uprising, which had called for the establishing of a revolutionary Commune. The government based in Versailles and led by Thiers refused to exchange him for hostages held by the Commune, feeling he presented too much of a threat. In the absence of Blanqui, his followers along with a strong contingent of neo-Jacobins made up the majority of the Commune, the majority that would press for dictatorial measures modeled on those of the Jacobin period of the French Revolution.

The opening shots of the Commune were fired on March 18, 1871, when forces under the leadership of Generals Lecomte and Thomas attempted to seize the cannons paid for and held by the workers of Montmartre. For the people, after the military defeat and the four-month siege, this was one insult too many, and the two generals were killed on the spot. The government of the republic no longer held sway in Paris and a provisional government led by the Central Committee of the National Guard governed until the elections on March 25, when the Paris Commune officially assumed power. The elections occurred in all of Paris's arrondissements, even the most bourgeois, though none of those elected from the wealthier districts agreed to sit on the Commune. In the end, seventy men did, including twenty-five workers. In effect, Paris had seceded from France.

The young Commune (made up of men inexperienced in politics but battle-hardened in the revolution in which they had been uncompromising fighters against the dictatorship of Napoleon III) set out immediately to construct a new society. The guillotine was burned, the standing army was abolished, and separation of church and state was declared, along with the suppression of the religious budget. Goods held in pawnshops were liberated, rents were rolled back and the payment of debts owed were suspended. The members of the Commune were subject to recall and were only paid 600 francs. Night work for bakers was banned, easing the lives an important sector of the Parisian working class.

Versailles had early demonstrated its viciousness, summarily killing Communards taken prisoner. On April 5, the Commune issued its decree on hostages, stating, "If, continuing to fail to recognize the customary conditions of war between civilized peoples our enemies massacre yet one more of our soldiers, we will answer with the execution of either the same or twice the number of prisoners." The Commune was already holding Darboy, the archbishop of Paris, as a hostage and had offered to exchange him along with a number of other hostages for Blanqui, but the Versaillais had refused the bargain, to dire consequences.

The Commune did not just concern itself with substantive measures; it also recognized the importance of symbols, ordering the dismantling of the Vendôme Column, a symbol of the military might of Napoleon I made from the melting of captured cannons. This decision was carried out on May 16, less than two weeks before the death of the Commune; its organizer, the great artist Gustave Courbet, was held responsible for it and made to pay 323,000 francs in indemnity. Shortly before the destruction of the column, the Commune had also ordered the destruction of the Chapelle Expiatoire, built to atone for execution of the French monarch during the Great Revolution. The Commune was thus both a symbolic and a substantive rupture with France's reactionary past.

In the important battle beyond the symbolic, the Commune failed miserably. On March 21, just three days after the killing of Generals Lecomte and Thomas, the republican forces of Versailles began their attack. After much debate over whether the fight should be taken to the enemy (which risked appearing aggressive) or waiting for the attacks to come, a sortie was ordered on April 3 that ended in disaster for the Commune. The Versaillais slowly managed to capture all the forts surrounding Paris, bombarding the city all the while. They entered the city's gates on May 21, beginning the *Semaine Sanglante* (Bloody Week) that ended the first experiment in worker rule. The Versaillais had to take the city street by street, barricade by barricade; in the midst of this attack, the Commune, which had avoided carrying out the threat made in its decree on the hostages, executed its forty-seven hostages (including Archbishop Darboy) on May 24.

On May 28, the final fighters made their stand at Père Lachaise Cemetery, at a spot that now bears their name, Le Mur des Fédérés (The Wall of the Federals) near which the leaders of the French working-class movement are buried, and before

4

which wreaths are placed by every French left-wing party on May Day. Twenty thousand Communards were killed during the Bloody Week and its aftermath; thousands more were imprisoned, deported, and exiled. The French working class was crushed and defeated for decades, not recovering until the mid-1890s.

Why did this occur? Why did the Commune fail? This is the great topic of the participants in the discussion carried out in the pages of the great literary review *La Revue Blanche* twenty-six years after the defeat, a large excerpt of which is included here. The journal, whose contributors over its lifetime were among the greatest writers in Europe, also published important political articles, and the "Investigation into the Commune" is perhaps the most fascinating autopsy of a failed revolution we have. If for those of us living nearly 150 years after the event it was one worthy of nearly sacred awe, for those involved in its life and death it was the work of noble but flawed men. The participants in the discussion are open about the error of not seizing the money held by the Bank of France, about the Commune having spent too much time deliberating on ancillary issues and not concentrating on the military front, on the splits in the Commune between the minority and the majority over the issue of the Committee of Public Safety. These interpretations are perhaps the most valid ones: only these men and women knew the difficult realities the Commune faced, only they lived through a fight that was not a matter of theory but rather of life or death.

Militants and thinkers in the decades since have drawn various lessons, some (like the Bolsheviks) leading to results far more disastrous in the long run than those taken by the Commune: the Commune stands an example even today, which cannot be said about the Bolsheviks. In fact, one of France's most important contemporary philosophers, Michel Onfray, few of whose works have been translated into English, describes the left he is part of as the "Communard left," a democratic, libertarian left that doesn't follow any leaders.

There is no way to tell what would have happened had the Commune survived, or of it ever had a chance of holding out against the rest of France, since the Communes formed in other major cities failed to thrive. We know the strategy they chose failed, but we don't know that any other would have succeeded. It never got a chance to fully carry out its experiment. Nor did it ever sully its name, despite the attempts by its enemies to do so through their condemnation of the executions of hostages it carried out as it was dying. That is its tragedy and its glory.

To learn more about the Commune:

We are extremely poorly served in English when it comes to the Paris Commune. Alistair Horne's *The Fall of Paris* is, like all his books, marvelously well written and gives a through portrait of the Franco-Prussian war, the siege, and the Commune. Reading it will allow readers of Karl Marx's *The Civil War in France*, *the* classic analysis of the event, to understand who the players were and the total context.

P.-O. Lissagaray's *The History of the Paris Commune of 1871* is the most famous of the historical accounts by a participant. It's essential, thorough, and will probably confuse most readers who don't have a reasonably in-depth knowledge of the republican movement in France under Napoleon III. That said, no book better defends the Commune.

In late 2014 John Merriman, already the author of an excellent book on the propagandists by the deed, *The Dynamite Club*, published perhaps the best popular account of the Commune we will have, *Massacre*. Sympathetic to the Commune, it isn't blind to its failures and failings, and the book's portrayal of day-to-day life during the Commune's brief life is lucid and clear-eyed. As its title indicates a large portion of the book, perhaps too large, is dedicated to the military side of the Commune's existence and the brutality of its crushing rather than its social aspects and aspiration, but this is just a quibble. It belongs on the bookshelves of anyone interested in the Commune.

Louise Michel's memoirs, *The Red Virgin*, dedicate too few pages to the Commune, but they are beautifully written pages. Her book on the Commune itself is both disappointing and not available in English.

For a specifically anarchist perspective, Andrew Zonnefeld's anthology *The Commune: Paris 1871* brings together an interesting selection of opinions about the Commune by some of the movement's great figures, including Bakunin, Kropotkin, Louise Michel, Alexander Berkman, and Voltairine de Cleyre.

Strangely, we can find the most interesting and approachable books in this area in the realm of fiction. Jules Vallès's novel *L'insurgé* (*The Insurrectionist*), the third volume of his autobiographical trilogy, is a thrilling, barely fictionalized account of his experience as a member of the Commune and the International, and its most important journalist. It's out of print but is worth hunting down. If there's one book to be read about the Commune, this is it.

Jean Vautrin's novel *The Cry of the People*, written about fifteen years ago, also provides an exciting and tragic account of the revolution. Vautrin is unabashedly of the left, and his sympathy for the life of the French working class, a feature of most of his novels, is put to effective use here.

Peter Watkins's monumental film *The Commune (Paris, 1871)* is essential viewing. Unapologetically pro-Commune, made in faux-documentary style, it succeeds in providing a feel for the sweep and majesty of the Commune's brief existence.

Finally, Bertolt Brecht's seldom-performed epic play *The Days of the Commune* presents the debates and heroism of the Commune in a clear, didactic, partisan theatrical form. An interesting version of it, directed by Zoe Beloff, was performed on the streets of New York over the course of several months in 2012, and a film version of it can be seen at www.daysofthecommune.com.

■ TIMELINE OF THE CIVIL WAR IN FRANCE

1870

January 10 Approximately one hundred thousand people demonstrate against Bonaparte's Second Empire after the death of Victor Noir, a republican journalist killed by the Emperor's cousin, Pierre Bonaparte.

May 8 A national plebiscite votes confidence in the Empire with about 84 percent of votes in favor. On the eve of the plebiscite, members of the Paris Federation were arrested on a charge of conspiring against Napoleon III. This pretext was further used by the government to launch a campaign of persecution of the members of the International throughout France.

July 19 After a diplomatic struggle over the Prussian attempt for the Spanish throne, Louis Bonaparte declares war on Prussia.

July 23: Marx completes what will become known as his "First Address."

July 26: The "First Address" is approved and internationally distributed by the General Council of the International Working Men's Association.

August 4–6 Crown Prince Frederick, commanding one of the three Prussian armies invading France, defeats French Marshal MacMahon at Worth and Weissenburg, pushes him out of Alsace (northeastern France), surrounds Strasbourg, and drives on toward Nancy. The other two Prussian armies isolate Marshal Bazaine's forces in Metz.

August 16–18 French Commander Bazaine's efforts to break his soldiers through the German lines are bloodily defeated at Mars-la-Tour and Gravelotte. The Prussians advance on Chalons.

September 1 Battle of Sedan. MacMahon and Bonaparte, attempting to relieve Bazaine at Metz and finding the road closed, enter battle and are defeated at Sedan.

September 2 Emperor Napoleon III and Marshal MacMahon capitulate at Sedan with more than eighty-three thousand soldiers.

September 4 At the news of Sedan, Paris workers invade the Palais Bourbon and force the Legislative Assembly to proclaim the fall of the Empire. By evening, the Third Republic is proclaimed at the Hôtel de Ville (the City Hall) in Paris. The provisional Government of National Defense (GND) is established to continue the war effort to remove Germany from France.

September 5 A series of meetings and demonstrations begin in London and other big cities, at which resolutions and petitions are passed demanding that the British government immediately recognize the French Republic. The General Council of the First International take a direct part in the organization of this movement.

September 6 GND issues a statement blaming the war on the Imperial government. It now wants peace, but "not an inch of our soil, not a stone of our fortresses, will we cede." With Prussia occupying Alsace-Lorraine, the war does not stop.

September 19 Two German armies begin the long siege of Paris. Bismarck figures the "soft and decadent" French workers will quickly surrender. The GND sends a delegation to Tours, soon to be joined by Gambetta (who escapes from Paris in a balloon), to organize resistance in the provinces.

October 27 French army, led by Bazaine with 140,000–180,000 men at Metz, surrenders.

October 30 French National Guard is defeated at Le Bourget.

October 31 Upon the receipt of news that the Government of National Defense had decided to start negotiations with the Prussians, Paris workers and revolutionary sections of the National Guard rise up in revolt, led by Blanqui. They seize the Hôtel de Ville and set up their revolutionary government—the Committee of Public Safety, headed by Blanqui.

On October 31, Gustave Flourens prevents any members of the Government of National Defense from being shot, as had been demanded by one of the insurrectionists.

November 1 Under pressure from the workers, the Government of National Defense promises to resign and schedule national elections to the Commune—promises it has no intention of keeping. With the workers pacified by their "legal" charade, the government violently seizes the Hôtel de Ville and reestablishes its domination over the besieged city. Paris official Blanqui is arrested for treason.

1871

January 22 The Paris proletariat and the National Guards hold a revolutionary demonstration, initiated by the Blanquists. They demand the overthrow of the government and the establishment of a Commune. By order of the Government of National Defense, the Breton Mobile Guard, which was defending the Hôtel de Ville, opens fire on the demonstrators. After massacring the unarmed workers, the government begins preparations to surrender Paris to the Germans.

January 28 After four long months of workers' struggle, Paris is surrendered to the Prussians. While all regular troops are disarmed, the National Guard is permitted to keep their arms—the population of Paris remains armed and allows the occupying armies only a small section of the city.

February 8 Elections are held in France, unknown to most of the nation's population.

February 12 New National Assembly opens at Bordeaux; two thirds of members are conservatives and wish the war to end.

February 16 The Assembly elects Adolphe Thiers chief executive.

February 26 The preliminary peace treaty between France and Germany signed at Versailles by Thiers and Jules Favre, on the one hand, and Bismarck, on the other. France surrenders Alsace and East Lorraine to Germany and pays it indemnities to the sum of five billion francs. German army of occupation slowly withdraws as indemnity payments made. The final peace treaty is signed in Frankfort-on-Main on May 10, 1871.

March 1–3 After months of struggle and suffering, Paris workers react angrily to the entry of German troops in the city and the ceaseless capitulation of the government. The National Guard defects and organizes a Central Committee.

March 10 The National Assembly passes a law on the deferred payment of overdue bills; under this law the payment of debts on obligations concluded between August 13 and November 12, 1870 could be deferred. Thus, the law leads to the bankruptcy of many petty bourgeoisie.

March 11 The Assembly adjourns. With trouble in Paris, it establishes its government at Versailles on March 20.

March 18 Adolphe Thiers attempts to disarm Paris and sends French troops (regular army), but the workers of Montmartre, who had paid for the cannons, refuse to turn them over. Generals Claude Martin Lecomte and Jacques Leonard Clement Thomas are killed by crowd. Many troops peacefully withdraw; some remain in Paris. With Thiers outraged, the Civil War begins.

March 26 A municipal council—the Paris Commune—is elected by the citizens of Paris. Commune consists of workers, among them members of the First International and followers of Proudhon and Blanqui.

March 28 The Central Committee of the National Guard, which up to then had carried on the government, resigns after it first decrees the permanent abolition of the "Morality Police."

March 30 The Commune abolishes conscription and the standing army; the National Guard, in which all citizens capable of bearing arms are to be enrolled, becomes the sole armed force. The Commune remits all payments of rent for dwelling houses from October 1870 until April 1871. On the same day the foreigners elected to the Commune are confirmed in office, because "the flag of the Commune is the flag of the World Republic."

April 1 The Commune declares that the highest salary received by any member of the Commune does not exceed 6,000 francs.

April 2 In order to suppress the Paris Commune, Thiers appeals to Bismarck for permission to supplement the Versailles Army with French prisoners of war, most of whom had been serving in the armies that surrendered at Sedan and Metz. In return for the five billion francs indemnity payment, Bismarck agrees. The French army begins siege of Paris. Paris is continually bombarded, moreover, by the very people who had stigmatized as a sacrilege the bombardment of the same city by the Prussians.

The Commune decrees the separation of the church from the state and the abolition of all state payments for religious purposes as well as the transformation of all church property into national property. Religion is declared a purely private matter.

April 5 Decree on hostages adopted by the Commune in an attempt to prevent Communards from being shot by the French government. Under this decree, all persons found guilty of being in contact with the French government are declared hostages. This decree is never carried out.

April 6 The guillotine is brought out by the 137th Battalion of the National Guard and publicly burnt, amid great popular rejoicing.

April 7 On April 7, the French army captures the Seine crossing at Neuilly, on the western front of Paris.

Reacting to French government policy of shooting captured Communards, the Commune issues an "eye-for-an-eye" policy statement, threatening retaliation. The bluff is quickly called; Paris workers execute no one.

April 8 A decree excluding all religious symbols from the schools— pictures, dogmas, prayers, in a word, "all that belongs to the sphere of the individual's conscience." The decree is gradually applied.

April 11 In an attack on southern Paris the French army is repelled with heavy losses by General Eudes.

April 12 The Commune decides that the Victory Column on the Place Vendôme, which had been cast from guns captured by Napoleon after the war of 1809, should be dismantled as a symbol of chauvinism and incitement to national hatred. This decree is carried out on May 16.

April 16 The Commune announces the postponement of all debt obligations for three years and abolition of interest on them.

The Commune orders a statistical tabulation of factories which had been closed down by the manufacturers, and the working out of plans for the carrying on of these factories by workers formerly employed in them, who are to be organized in cooperative societies, and also plans for the organization of these cooperatives in one great union.

April 20 The Commune abolishes night work for bakers, and also abolishes the workers' registration cards, which since the Second Empire had been run as a monopoly by men named by the police—exploiters of the first rank; the issuing of these registration cards is transferred to the mayors of the twenty arrondissements of Paris.

April 23 Thiers breaks off the negotiations for the exchange, proposed by Commune, of the Archbishop of Paris [Georges Darboy] and a number of other priests held hostages in Paris, for only one man, Blanqui, who had twice been elected to the Commune but is a prisoner in Clairvaux.

April 27 In sight of the impending municipal elections of April 30, Thiers enacts one of his great conciliation scenes. He exclaims from the tribune of the Assembly, "There exists no conspiracy against the republic but that of Paris, which compels us to shed French blood. I repeat it again and again." Out of seven hundred thousand municipal councilors, the united Legitimists, Orleanists, and Bonapartists (Party of Order) do not carry eight thousand.

April 30 The Commune orders the closing of the pawnshops on the ground that they are a private exploitation of labor, and are in contradiction with the right of the workers to their instruments of labor and to credit.

May 5 The Commune orders the demolition of the Chapel of Atonement, which had been built in expiation of the execution of Louis XVI.

May 9 Fort Issy, which is completely reduced to ruins by gunfire and constant French bombardment, is captured by the French army.

May 10 The peace treaty concluded in February is now signed, known as the Treaty of Frankfurt (endorsed by National Assembly on May 18).

May 16 The Victory Column at Place Vendôme is pulled down.

May 21–28 Versailles troops enter Paris on May 21. The Prussians who held the northern and eastern forts allow the Versailles troops to advance across the land north of the city, which was forbidden ground to them under the armistice—Paris workers held the flank with only weak forces. As a result of this, only a weak resistance was put up in the western half of Paris, in the luxury city, while it grew stronger and more tenacious the nearer the Versailles troops approached the eastern half, the working-class city.

The French army spends eight days massacring workers, shooting civilians on sight. The operation is led by Marshal MacMahon, who would later become president of France. Tens of thousands of Communards and workers are summarily executed, as many as thirty thousand. Thirty-eight thousand others are imprisoned and seven thousand are forcibly deported.

Timeline courtesy of the Marxists Internet Archive.

■ JULES VALLÈS

PARIS, FREE CITY

There is the working bourgeoisie and the parasitic bourgeoisie.

Those who *Le Cri du Peuple* attacks, who its editors have everywhere and always attacked, are the do-nothings, those who traffic in positions and have turned politics into a trade.

They're a herd of chatterboxes, a mass of ambitious men, a seedbed of subprefects and state counselors.

They produce nothing but froth. Through shadowy banking systems and shameful stock market speculations they grab the profits produced by those who work—they're shameless speculators who rob the poor and loan to kings, who played dice on the drums of Transnonain or December 2 and who are already thinking of ways to carve their bank out of the corpse of the bloodied fatherland.

But there is a *working* bourgeoisie, this one honest and valiant. It goes to the workshop wearing a cap, wanders in wooden clogs through the mud of factories, in the cold and the heat remains at its cash register or its office, in its small shop or its large factory, behind the windows of a boutique or the walls of a manufactory. It swallows dust and smoke, burns itself behind the workbench or the forge, helps out wherever needed. It is, with its courage and fears, the sister of the proletariat.

For it has its fears, its risks of failure, its days when bills come due. Thanks precisely to those parasites who need trouble and agitation in order to live, not one fortune is certain today.

First published in *Le Cri du Peuple*, March 22, 1871.

Nothing is stable: today's boss is tomorrow's laborer, and school graduates see their jackets worn to rags.

How many I know among those who are well established and well dressed, who have the same worries as the poor, who sometimes ask what will become of their children and who would trade all their chances of happiness and profit for the certainty of a modest job and a tearless old age.

It is this whole world of workers who fear ruin and unemployment who make up Paris, the great Paris. Why in all our misery as men and citizens wouldn't they take each other by the hand? And why, in this solemn moment, wouldn't we try for once and for all to wrest this country—where we are brothers in effort and danger—from that eternal uncertainty which allows adventurers to forever succeed, and obliges honest men to forever suffer and tremble!

Fraternity was queen the other day before the cannons and under the bright sun. It must remain queen and Paris must take a solemn decision—a decision that will be the only correct one and will only take its place in history if it manages to avoid civil war and returns to the war against the victorious Bismarck.

As for ourselves, we are ready to impose nothing, to suffer everything in this painful circle of fatality, on condition that the freedom of Paris remain safe and that the flag of the republic shelter, in an independent city, a courageous people of workers.

Workers and bourgeois: several hundred years ago, in that Germany from which the cannons that struck us came, four cities declared themselves free cities; for centuries they were great and proud, rich and peaceful. In all corners of the world they were heard, and they cast merchandise and gold on all shores!

In order to cut the Gordian knot that had bound together our recent misfortunes other than with the saber, there is only one message:

PARIS, FREE CITY!

Through the intermediary of the people's representatives we will *immediately* negotiate with the government of Versailles for a status quo without battle, and with the Prussians *for the settling of indemnities.*

No blood will be shed, the cannons will remain cold, the barracks will close, and the workshops reopen and work recommence.

Work starts anew! This is the inflexible necessity, the supreme desire. Let us all come to agreement so that everyone finds tomorrow his work. Citizens of all classes and ranks: this is salvation!

Paris, a free city, returns to its labors.

This secession would save the provinces from their fears and the *faubourgs* from famine.

Bordeaux said: Down with Paris!

We for our part cry out: Long live France, Long live Paris! And we promise to never extend to that France that slanders us the hand that they took as a threat.

It's between Montrouge and Montmartre that, whatever the circumstances, will always beat the heart of the country, which we'll always love and which will return to us in the end.

Several cities—precisely those feared by the moderates—can also negotiate so they can live free and take part in the great federation of republican cities.

To those who fear that they would suffer from isolation, we would respond that there are no frontiers high enough to prevent labor from crossing them, industry from razing them, commerce from poking holes in them.

Labor! The cities with high chimneys that spit the smoke of factories, with their great workshops and long counters; cities made fertile don't die! Even peasants don't kill the goose that lays the golden eggs!

Having a flag of its own, Paris could no longer be defamed or threatened, and it will remain the able seeker, the happy finder who invents beautiful plans and great instruments, who will be forever implored to put its seal on this metal or that cloth, on this toy or that weapon, on this cup or that basin, on the mould of a porcelain or the silk of a gown! It will remain master and king.

PARIS, FREE CITY

No more blood spilled! Rifles at rest! Mayors are named and magistrates elected. And then to work! To work! The bell tolls for work and not for combat.

THE ELECTION

The elections have taken place.

The act of popular sovereignty was performed in a city bristling with men in arms, shining with bayonets, and bruised by cannon wheels.

In the midst of this military gear it voted, serene and threatening, depositing its cannonballs in the ballot box. But passing through these lines of sentinels, this camp standing around a red flag, liberty suffered not a single wound, not one!

It is now one week that this "minority" of pillagers and assassins holds Paris under its rifle butt.

Who has this rifle struck? Has it crushed a head? Smashed a window?

Answer, wretches! Answer, imbeciles!

You wanted to put the republic on a stretcher; we had it borne on a shield. What was supposed to be a battle was a festival.

It is up to us that every day of social childbirth have this grandeur and joy; to us and to you, who aren't going force us to beat the charge on our drums, right?

And starting tomorrow we will see at work the slandered and the wounded that make up the victorious list, full of unknown names, just as the Assembly of the Third Estate was full of men who made what the world calls the French Revolution.

First published in *Le Cri du Peuple*, March 29, 1871.

OUR PEOPLE

They held out against an army. Before these improvised soldiers the General Staff of illustrious generals was forced to line up, worried and grave, trembling and desperate!

All those victors of Algeria and Mexico, those who triumphed in Italy, that whole old plumed world, covered in spittle and glory had to remain silent.

Constables and gendarmes had to be signed up at so much a head, at three francs a day; rehabilitation had to be promised to the bohemia of Legitimacy and the Empire; it was necessary to distribute crosses to these and to promise posts to those in order to obtain a forward march for the removal of a few barricades and the conquering of a few positions. My god, yes!

What can be said of these poor victories! What do they prove once we realize that at the last minute the *fédérés* suddenly shook loose the triumph, and that there was hesitation and disarray among those captains who saw those civic battalions come on, return and return again, indomitable and proud, ready to be mowed down rather than lower their flag before the enemy!

The Revolution is safe! Nothing that the calculations of treason or the hazards of battle could bring can do anything in the future against republican Paris. Even if a million men were to pass over these paving stones they couldn't crush the harvest!

Look then! These insurgents were called gypsies and bandits! Their generals were possessed of the *sang froid* of heroes, and from their smashed faces they have spit their blood in the face of the assassins!

Not a single example of hesitation or weakness has been cited! Duval, Henry, Flourens, and all the others laughed in the face of their executioners!

Such chiefs have never been seen; unknown chiefs issued from the people. What mattered the taking of this redoubt, the conquest of that field, the occupation of that hill?

It was a question of showing that with neither plan nor discipline the people knew how to face up to the strategists and statesmen; that a corner of the world called Paris put the entire

First published in *Le Cri du Peuple*, April 7, 1871.

past, monarchical, clerical, and military in its place and thwarted it! It was necessary to cook something up, to lie and betray in order to have the appearance of winning for a day!

Noble Paris! Proud city! Throng of heroes!

How sad and proud they looked today behind Henry's coffin, he who was killed from afar by the fire of Mont-Valérien.

"Vengeance!" said some.

"We only want justice," said most of them.

And the very father of the victim asked that the assassins of his son be forgiven! Perhaps at that very moment Gallifet and his drunken officers amused themselves with the agonies of our people and laughingly recounted how they had executed our men before a firing squad and then crushed them under their boots by the corner of a wall!

Will this last long? Paris must declare itself!

Will it be the march on Versailles? Will it be the freeing of Paris?

FREE PARIS

We will return to this, like Cato and Carthage! Every day, until our tongues have been cut out.

We can all agree on this! But we must hurry!

We must hurry, because the people are sometimes subject to terrible furies that demand fearful reprisals.

They are given the example of crime: prisoners slaughtered and wounded, men who are finished off! And if it were to see red tomorrow and call for a head for a head, an eye for an eye, a tooth for a tooth?!

Men of feeling, honest men, republicans, you must hurry!

Do you want a Paris that is a free city, a happy city? Or do you want a furious Paris, even if it has been crushed and defeated?

Let's go! Let the upper floors and the lower floors come to terms and make peace within the next two days. Whoever works: small boss, poor worker, forward and live! We want our freedom!
. . . Or death!

And in keeping with the answer given we will join together, in labor or in combat!

Time is passing, and blood overflows, the blood of our people! But it is time to close the wound!

FREE PARIS!

THE DEAD

The people who today saw our dead pass by will never forgive! Between them and the killers there is an abyss of hatred and fear dug as deep as the enormous pit into which the corpses were lowered.

The very ones who were frightened by the red flags that floated over the black catafalques will remember the ominous burial of April 6, and the men of Versailles, whatever may happen, will live cloaked in a silent and somber reprobation that will follow them, too, to the cemetery—whether they arrive by the glorious route of the Capitol, or arrive mutilated from the Tarpeian rocks!

Not a cry could be heard above that crowd that rolled like a black and silent river on all sides of the hearses, but everywhere could be heard the murmuring of a horrible, deliberate, and threatening pain.

If the men of Versailles had seen this convoy pass by they would have been seized either by a silent fear or an immense regret! On the path followed by the mortuary cart a curse will forever rise up against them—a formless and disarmed revolt, but one that will blow upon their dishonored faces like the sigh of a breeze of death!

The more corpses you pile up, and the more triumphs like this one come your way, the longer will be the lament and the more horribly it will weigh upon this mass grave!

Revolutionary hope remains alive even in our mourning!

But ashen mothers could be found there, bowed over cut-off coffins that had been guillotined by saws so that the heads of the dead could be seen.

One of these mothers had found her son. Another didn't know if she recognized hers in a pile of broken, eyeless, toothless flesh that bled black on the white wood!

Twenty of them were laid out like that! Some in the shirts of the poor, frayed and full of holes; others had fine clothes. Plebeian and bourgeois mixed together in the sepulcher as they had been in combat!

First published in *Le Cri du Peuple*, April 8, 1871.

Even as we were leaving, more arrived in the straw at the bottom of a bus!

Perhaps tomorrow even more will be brought, ten times more!

Nevertheless, the music of the bugles gave chills today! How sad and heartrending; it seemed to sound for the living as well as the dead!

Père Lachaise is a cemetery, but Paris is a tomb where they will be buried alive if they are victorious, and which will refuse their cadavers if they are defeated!

Tonight the bayonets glistened hard and somber under the gray sky, and there were flashes of terrible sadness in the tearless eyes!

THE PEOPLE OF BELLEVILLE

The 191st Battalion, commanded by Citizen Lecomte, returned yesterday from the Fort d'Issy, where it had been for eight days.

It passed thought the Place de l'Hôtel de Ville where members of the Commune went to receive it and congratulate it on its excellent conduct.

It brought back as a trophy a red cover that had served as its flag and was full of bullet holes.

A member of the Commune from the nineteenth arrondissement led this glorious battalion back to Belleville and thanked it for its devotion to the Commune and the Republic.

It was beautiful to see these guards resting among their families, and ready to respond to a new call from the Commune.

The 114th Battalion from the nineteenth arrondissement had already given an example of firmness and civic courage at the Neuilly roundabout.

With four hundred men it held this important point under the fire of Mont-Valérien and pushed back several attacks by the Versaillais.

All honor to these battalions.

Belleville proves by its acts its civic courage and its devotion to the Commune.

First published in *Le Cri du Peuple*, April 14, 1871.

■ DEBATE IN THE COMMUNE ON THE HOSTAGES AND THE COMMITTEE OF PUBLIC SAFETY

Like any good French government, the Commune had its Journal Officiel, *in which were published government decrees, notices, foreign news, financial reports, death notices, and starting with the issue of April 15, minutes of the meetings of the Commune. Many of the most important revolutionary propagandists of the time participated in its publication, including Pierre Vésinier and Maxime Vuillaume, a feat all the more astounding because along with the* Journal Officiel *they also published their own newspapers during the same period.*

After the death of the Commune, many survivors mocked the journal's excessive parliamentarism and, given the circumstances, the discussions there are a mix of the ridiculous and the sublime. We find discussions of the delegates to be sent to attend a funeral as well as the debate on the postponing of the payment of debts due; discussions of the changing of place names and of the legitimacy of elections with insufficient participants. The minutes are frequently cut off abruptly as the Commune entered into secret session.

Translated here are the minutes of one of the stormiest of the Commune's sessions. On May 17 the discussion revolved around two principal subjects: the executions of the hostages held by the Commune and a letter of the minority of the Commune, largely members of the International, protesting against the extraordinary powers granted the Committee of Public Safety. The discussion was so lengthy that its publication required two issues. The text that follows is the contents of the minority's letter.

At the session that was to have taken place Monday, May 15, the members belonging to the minority of the Commune had resolved to read a declaration that would doubtless have made the political misunderstandings that existed in the assembly disappear.

The absence of almost all the members of the majority did not permit the opening of the session.

It is thus our duty to enlighten public opinion concerning our attitude and to make known the points that separate us from the majority.

The members present: Arthur Arnould, Ostyn, Longuet, Arnold,[1] Lefrançais, Serraillier, Jules Vallès, Courbet, Victor Clément, Jourde, Varlin.[2]

DECLARATION

By a special and clear vote, the Paris Commune has abdicated its power into the hands of a dictatorship to which it has given the name of Public Safety.

The majority of the Paris Commune declared itself irresponsible by its vote and abandoned all responsibility in our current situation to this committee.

The minority to which we belong on the contrary affirms this idea, that the Commune at the politically and socially revolutionary moment must accept all responsibilities and decline none, however worthy might be the hands into which they will be abandoned.

For our part, we, like the majority, desire the carrying out of social and political renewal, but contrary to their ideas we demand, in the name of the suffrage we represent, the right to respond for ourselves for our acts before our voters, without

---

1. Georges Arnold (1837–1912)—Architect. Member of the Central Committee of the National Guard. Member of the Commune for the eighteenth arrondissement. Sentenced to deportation to New Caledonia, he designed buildings there and was an architect for the city of Paris upon his return from deportation.
2. Eugène Varlin (1839–1871)—Bookbinder. Leader of the International. Member of the Commune, elected by three arrondissements, serving for the sixth. Member of several commissions. Served on the barricades during the Bloody Week and attempted to prevent the execution of the hostages on the Rue Haxo. Captured on May 28 and summarily executed, shouting "Vive la République! Vive la Commune!"

hiding behind a supreme dictatorship that our mandate permits us neither to accept nor recognize.

And so we will only attend the assembly on the day it constitutes itself as a court of justice to judge one of its members.

Devoted to our great communal cause for which so many citizens die each day, we retire to our too neglected arrondissements. Convinced in any case that the question of war is more important than all others, we will pass the time our municipal functions allow us among our brothers of the National Guard and we will play our part in the decisive struggle carried out in the name of the people's rights.

Here too we will usefully serve our convictions and will avoid creating the splits in the Commune that we all condemn, persuaded that, majority or minority, despite our political divergences, we are all pursuing the same goals: political freedom and the emancipation of the workers.

Long Live the Social Republic!

Long Live the Commune!

Ch. Beslay,[3] Jourde, Theisz,[4] Lefrançais, Eugène Girardin, Vermorel, Clémence, Andrieu, Seraillier, Longuet, Arthur Arnould, Victor Clément, Avrail, Ostyn, Frankel, Pindy, Arnold, J. Vallès, Tridon, Varlin, Courbet.

Session of May 17, 1871

Presided over by Citizen Leo Meillet, seconded by Citizen Dr. Pillot

The session is opened at 2:30 P.M.

---

3. Charles Beslay (1795–?)—Engineer. Close friend and follower of Proudhon. Member of the International. Elder of the Commune, elected by the sixth arrondissement. On the finance commission he ensured that the money held by the Bank of France wasn't touched: "I went to the bank with the intention of protecting it from violence on the part of the extremist party of the Commune." Acquitted of all charges against him after the fall of the Commune. In later years adopted a "liberal socialism."

4. Albert Theisz (1839–1881)—Bronze carver. Member of the International. Member of the Commune for the eighteenth arrondissement (also elected by the twelfth). Member of the labor commission. Fought on the barricades during the Bloody Week. Sentenced to death in absentia. Participated in the International's activities in London while in exile. Worked at Rochefort's *L'Intransigeant* upon his return to France in 1880.

In conformity with the notice inserted in this morning's *Journal Officiel* a roll call by name is proceeded to by Citizen Amouroux,[5] one of the secretaries and a member of the Commune. Sixty-six members are present.

Citizen President: There will be reading of the minutes of the session of May 12.

The minutes are read and adopted without observations.

Citizen President gives a reading of a letter from Citizen Sicard,[6] resigning as member of the war commission.

The assembly gathers as a secret committee to hear a communication from Citizen Ferré,[7] delegate for general security.

The open session begins again at 3:15 P.M.

Citizen Urbain[8] communicates to the assembly a report by Lieutenant Butin, denouncing the rape and massacre of a female ambulance assistant while she was taking care of the wounded.

Citizen Urbain: This report is certified by Lieutenant Urbain of the 3rd Company of the 105th Battalion. I demand that either the Commune or the Committee of Public Safety decide that ten of the hostages we have in our hands be executed within twenty-four hours as reprisals for the murders of the nurse and of our parliamentarian who was greeted by a fusillade in contempt of

5. Charles Amouroux (1847–1885)—Hatmaker. Freemason. Member of the International. Member Commune representing the fourth arrondissement. Member of the external relations commission. Captured during the Bloody Week, he received three sentences to deportation. In New Caledonia volunteered to serve in the French forces fighting the native rebels.

6. Auguste Sicard (1839–after 1911)—Crinoline maker. Member of the Commune for the seventh arrondissement. Said to be "the soul of the administration of the seventh arrondissement." At the barricades on March 18. Supporter of the Committee of Public Safety. Sentenced to deportation. Lived in exile in London.

7. Théophile Ferré (1846–1871)—Militant Blanquist and accountant. Member of the Commune elected by the eighteenth arrondissement. Assistant prosecutor of the Commune. Tried and sentenced to death, he told his judges, "I lived free and I intend to die the same way." Executed November 28, 1871.

8. Raoul Urbain (1851–1902)—Schoolteacher. Member of the Commune for the seventeenth arrondissement. Member of the education commission. Opponent of religious schools and supporter of the execution of the hostages. Captured after the fall of the Commune and sentenced to forced labor for life in a penal colony. Later active in the cooperative movement.

the laws of men. I demand that five of these hostages be solemnly executed inside Paris before a delegation of all the battalions, and that the other five be executed at the advanced positions in front of the guardsmen who witnessed the murder.

Citizen J.-B. Clément: I support Citizen Urbain's proposal. I have information from a relative who has returned from Versailles where he was a prisoner. Our men who are detained in Versailles are badly mistreated; they are given very little bread, they are insulted, and they are struck with rifles butts. This must end. On this subject I will address a question to Citizen Parisel, head of the scientific delegation.

Citizen Parisel: I demand the floor.

Several members: A secret committee!

The assembly meets as a secret committee.

The public session resumes.

Citizen Rigault,[9] prosecutor of the Commune: I present the following proposal. Given its urgency the Commune decrees:

> Article 1. For those accused of political crimes and misdemea-
> nors, the jury of accusation can provisionally pronounce
> sentence immediately after having pronounced on the
> guilt of the accused.
> Article 2. The sentences shall be pronounced by a majority
> of votes.
> Article 3. These sentences shall be carried out within 24 hours.
> Raoul Rigault, Urbain, L. Chalain[10]

In my opinion we should answer the murders by the Versaillais in the most energetic fashion by striking the guilty and not the first people we see. Yet I must say that I'd rather allow

---

9. Raoul Rigault (1846–1871)—Student, journalist. Prosecutor and member of the Commune for the eighth arrondissement. Intimately involved in the hostage question, he ordered the execution of at least nine men during the Bloody Week. Accused of the setting of several fires. Arrested May 24 he was executed immediately. Also sentenced to death in absentia in June 1872.
10. Louis Chalain (1845–1895)—Lathe operator. Freemason. Member of the International and the Commune, representing the seventeenth arrondissement. Served as a police informant in Switzerland while in exile after the fall of the Commune.

guilty men to escape than to strike a single innocent man. Among the people we've detained there are true criminals who deserve to be considered as more than hostages. Well then, chance can very well designate the least guilty, and those who are the guiltiest might be spared. While waiting for justice to be completely established I have thought it useful to establish a tribunal charged with examining the crimes in question. What is more, I declare that I will request that the prescriptions for crimes of this kind not be taken into account. And I put on the same level both the men who are in agreement with Versailles and Bonaparte's accomplices.

Citizen President: There is a proposal formulated by Citizen Urbain.

Citizen Urbain: If the assembly decides that the reprisals will take place within a short time . . .

Citizen Raoul Rigault, prosecutor of the Commune: The jury of accusation is assigned for the day after tomorrow.

Citizen Urbain: If we are given the means to carry out the reprisals legally, and in an appropriate and prompt fashion, then I will be satisfied.

Citizen President: Here is the Urbain proposal:

> Given the urgency of the situation, the Commune decrees that ten individuals designated by the jury of accusation shall be executed as punishment for the murders committed by the Versaillais, and in particular the murder of a nurse, executed by them in contempt of all human laws.
>
> Five of these hostages shall be executed inside Paris in the presence of the National Guard.
>
> The other five shall be executed at the advanced positions, as close as possible to the place where the crimes were committed.
>
> Urbain

Citizen Protot:[11] On the subject of the proposal presented by Citizen Rigault, I declare that the jury of accusation can only

---

11. Eugène Protot (1839–1921)—Lawyer. Member of the Commune, representing the seventeenth arrondissement, though also elected by the second arrondissement. Delegate for justice, he proposed that judges be elected by the National Guard. Sentenced to death in absentia. Of Blanquist tendencies, he was a fierce opponent of Marx.

decide on questions of fact, that there are no punishments for the crimes that Citizen Rigault is speaking of. We must thus determine the punishment they are subject to.

Citizen Amouroux: It is my opinion that we must carry out reprisals. A month ago we announced the carrying out of a proposal that put an end to the crimes committed by the Versaillais for a certain period. But since in the end we did nothing, the Versaillais have once again started killing our people. Before what is occurring, I ask what use we are making of the law on the hostages. Should we condemn those held as such? But do the Versaillais judge our National Guardsmen? They take them and kill them on the open road. Let us act! And for each of our murdered brothers, let us answer with a triple execution. We have hostages, and among them priests; let's strike these first, for these matter to them more than do soldiers.

Citizen Vaillant: I am, I must confess, in a difficult situation when I, incompetent in the serious question that occupies us, see the only two individuals in this assembly who are competent in this matter in complete disagreement. Would it not be good if Citizens Protot and Rigault were to come to an agreement and bring this to some kind of resolution?

Citizen Protot, delegate for justice: There is no resolution to take. The prosecutor of the Commune can bring before the first two sections of the jury of accusation the people to be judged.

Citizen Rigault, prosecutor of the Commune: Given the nature of the events, these means do not suffice.

Citizen Pillot, president:[12] Let us not lose sight of what is under discussion, that is, Urbain's proposal. The great question of the moment is that of annihilating our enemies. We are in a revolution and we must act as revolutionaries. We must establish a tribunal which judges and which has its decrees executed.

Citizen Urbain: Will the jury of accusation which we just spoke of function? If it must function then my proposal stands; if not, we would do better to vote on Rigault's proposal.

12. Jean-Jacques Pillot (1808–1877)—Ordained priest, though he never practiced. Neo-babouvist communist member of the International. Member of the Commune for the first arrondissement. Accused of having set the fires at the Louvre and the Tuileries. Sentenced to life imprisonment, he died in jail.

Citizen Philippe, delegate of the twelfth arrondissement: We are exposed to a terrible reactionary force. We must take energetic measures. We must let it be known that we are determined to smash all the obstacles they put up against the triumphant march of the revolution.

Citizen Urbain: If we vote on the Rigault proposal, I withdraw mine.

Citizen Vaillant: If your jury of accusation functions as it should there is no need for a special proposal. You only have to apply the Commune's decree relating to reprisals, declaring that Citizens Rigault and Protot are charged with its execution.

Citizen Protot, delegate for justice: If I could have spoken with the prosecutor of the Commune I would have shown him that it would take at least two weeks to put on trial all those accused of complicity with Versailles. Those tried in absentia should already be sentenced.

Citizen Raoul Rigault, prosecutor of the Commune: According to the criminal code, juries are not competent to judge those tried in absentia. It is necessary that your juries be a true revolutionary tribunal.

Citizen President again reads the proposal of Citizen Raoul Rigault: I am going to put this proposal to a vote.

Citizen Protot, delegate for justice: I request the postponement of the vote until tomorrow.

Citizen Régère:[13] Yes! Until tomorrow!

Citizen Leo Frankel:[14] Yes! Until tomorrow!

---

13. Dominique Régère (1816–1893)—Veterinarian. Member of the International. Member of the Commune for the fifth arrondissement. Member of the finance commission. Arrested after the fall of the Commune, claimed he only acted under pressure from his voters and attacked the Commune. Sentenced to deportation.

14. Leo Frankel (1844–1896)—Silversmith. Born in Hungary. Member of the International and the Commune, representing the thirteenth arrondissement. Responsible for many of the Commune's socialist measures, including the abolition of night work for bakers. At the Commune he said, "The revolution of March 18 was exclusively made by the workers. If we do nothing for this class . . . I don't see what the Commune's reason for being is." Wounded on the barricades during the Bloody Week he fled France and lived in various countries, fighting for socialism wherever he lived.

Citizen President: It is proposed to submit the different proposals to a commission composed of Citizens Protot and Rigault.

Citizen Régère: With a third party; I propose Citizen Paschal Grousset. (Various movements)

Citizen Protot: A decree of the Commune says that a chamber composed of twelve jurors will decide on the fate of those accused of complicity with Versailles. I demand that this decree be carried out.

Citizen Urbain: I demand that my proposal be put to a vote.

Citizen Protot, delegate for justice: The notices have been given to have the detainees brought before the jury of accusation.

Citizen Urbain: In that case, I go along with the motion, but I declare that if the decree isn't carried out, I will resubmit my motion in two days.

Citizen Amouroux, one of the secretaries, gives a reading of the following decree:

The Paris Commune

Considering that the government of Versailles openly tramples upon both the rights of humanity and of war; that it has rendered itself guilty of horrors which didn't even sully those who invaded French soil;

Considering that the representatives of the Paris Commune have the pressing duty of defending the honor and lives of two million inhabitants who have placed the protection of their fates in their hands; that it is essential that all measures called for by the situation be immediately taken;

Considering that politicians and magistrates must reconcile public safety with the respect for freedoms:

Decrees

Article 1. Any person accused of complicity with the government of Versailles shall immediately have a warrant issued and be arrested.

Article 2. A jury of accusation shall be established within twenty-four hours to learn of the crimes for which he is accused.

Article 3. The jury shall decide within twenty-four hours

Article 4. Any accused held as a result of the verdict of the jury of accusation shall be a hostage of the people of Paris.

Article 5. Any execution of a prisoner of war or supporter of the government of the Paris Commune will immediately be followed by the execution of triple that number of hostages held by virtue of Article 4, who will be designated by lot.

Article 6. Every prisoner of war shall be brought before the jury of accusation, which will decide if he will be immediately freed or held as a hostage.

Citizen President: Here is the motion that I am putting to a vote: "The Commune, referring to its decree of April 7, demands its immediate execution and passes to the motion."

The motion is adopted.

Citizen Paschal Grousset makes the following motion: Citizens, at the opening of the session we noted with pleasure, but not without surprise, that several members of this assembly can be found at their benches whose names are found at the bottom of a manifesto published yesterday by certain newspapers. Their manifesto announced that they would no longer participate in our sessions. I would first like to know if their presence among us is a rejection of the harmful act of which they are guilty. I don't accept that certain members of the Commune can fill the papers with a manifesto in which they announce a split, in which these new Girondins declare that they are withdrawing, not to the departments—which they can't do—but to the arrondissements . . . that they should then come, without explanation, without justification, take their seats in their regular places . . .

Voice: This is not a motion! (Noise, interruptions from different sides)

Citizen Paschal Grousset: This is a motion, a motion of a higher order. After having asked the minority for the reason for this conduct I request the right to present a few observations on the subject of its manifesto. The minority accuses the Commune of having abdicated its power into the hands of the Committee of Public Safety. It accuses us of evading the responsibilities that weigh upon us. And yet it knows full well that in concentrating power in the hands of five men who have its confidence to decide on the terrible necessities of the situation, the Commune in no way intended to abdicate. For our part at least, we accept full responsibility. We are united with the committee that we named, are accountable for its acts, are ready to support it to the bitter end, as long as it marches on the revolutionary road, and ready to strike and smash it if it deviates from it.

It is thus false that we abdicated.

It is even more false that the minority's manifesto was provoked by this so-called abdication. The proof of this is that this same minority took part in the vote on the naming of the second Committee of Public Safety; that Article 3, conferring plenary powers on the Committee of Public Safety already existed at the time of the vote; that the very definition of these plenary powers had at that time been adopted on the proposal of one of the members of the minority.

We thus have the right to say that Article 3 is not the real reason for the manifesto. We thus have the right to say that the real reason is the failure suffered by the minority in the choice of members of the committee and the revocation of the military commission that issued from its ranks. If the reasons it alleges were sincere, the minority should have formulated its protest before the renewal of the Committee of Public Safety, and not after having participated in the vote, which meant recognizing the principle.

Finally, the minority declares that it wants to move from the parliamentary role to action by entirely dedicating itself to the administration of the arrondissements. Of course, they will not reproach those of us here for not being supporters of this system.

Who opposed the parliamentary tendencies that came to light in this assembly? Who has always demanded brief and rare sessions, closed to the public, without speeches—action sessions? Who, if not this minority that noisily announces its withdrawal on the pretext that it can't act; who constantly, as much as it could, prevented us from acting?

Citizens, I conclude. If the members of the Commune who announced their withdrawal really intend to dedicate themselves to the arrondissements, I would say: all the better. That would be better than coming here and preventing courageous and resolute men from taking the measure that the situation demands and the responsibility for which they accept.

If, instead of keeping their promises, these members attempt maneuvers that may compromise the safety of the Commune they are deserting, we will seize and strike them.

As for us, we will do our duty. Until victory or death, we will remain at the combat post that the people entrusted us with.

Citizen Jules Vallès: We came here yesterday to declare to the assembly that we were ready to enter into discussions on the political differences that seem to divide us. Our sentiments are contrary to those Citizen Grousset seems to suppose we hold. I declare, for myself and my friends, that what we want in the Commune is the most perfect harmony.

Citizen P. Grousset, in reminding us that we voted the establishment of the Committee of Public Safety, forces us to say that we sacrificed our sentiments in the face of a bombarded Paris.

We saw a danger in Article 3 of the Commune's decree. We ask that all of us together investigate whether, instead of creating a weapon, you have created a threat. We ask that this be calmly discussed. In a word, we want all forces to come together to ensure our salvation.

For my part, I declared that it was necessary to come to an agreement with the Central Committee and the majority, but the minority must also be respected, which is also a force. In all sincerity, we declare to you that we want harmony within the Commune and that our withdrawal to the arrondissements is not a threat.

We ask that you place on the agenda for tomorrow a discussion in which we can examine the facts and ensure the gathering of all forces to march against the enemy.

Citizen Langevin:[15] I completely agree with the words of Citizen J. Vallès, but I protest against those of Citizen Paschal Grousset. I voted against the Committee of Public Safety, but the majority having established it, I accepted it. Nevertheless, I think

15. Camille Langevin (1843–1913)—Lathe operator. Member of the Commune for the fifteenth arrondissement. Sentenced to deportation, but had already fled France. Active in the cooperative movement after the amnesty.

I have the right to say that there is a serious danger in Article 3 of the decree, which places in its hands the nomination and removal of delegates. (Noise)

Citizen Miot:[16] Yesterday the minority carried out an act that was clearly hostile to the majority. Why did it not give and ask for explanations before making a decision? A serious accusation was made against us: they dare to say that we renounced the exercising of the mandate that was entrusted to us. This is not the case. Isn't absolute control reserved to the Commune in the decree that establishes the Committee of Public Safety? As author of the proposal I did all I could so that the authority of the Commune not be absorbed. Can you not revoke this Committee at your will when you come to think that its authority may be dangerous? I repeat: the minority carried out a regrettable act yesterday that the public severely judges and which it will have to account for to its voters.

Citizen Arnould:[17] I request a correction to the minutes of the last session published in the *Journal Officiel*; it has to do with this question that is stirring us up. The *Officiel* has me say: "If one of the motions proposed to you is adopted, the Commune will serve only to incriminate the members of the Committee of Public Safety when it judges this convenient, and it could very well never hold another session." This is as far from my thoughts as possible. What I said and mean is: "I will not fight the Billioray and Ferré amendments. I will vote for them, for they are the inevitable deduction from Article 3, establishing the Committee of Public Safety, and I will ask that the Commune, understanding the logic of its acts, cease its periodic meetings."

---

16. Jules Miot (1809–1883)—Pharmacist. Democratic socialist representative in 1848. Member of the International and the Commune, representing the nineteenth arrondissement. Member of the commission that proposed the establishing of the Committee of Public Safety. Sentenced to death in absentia. Politically active in exile, though he withdrew from politics upon his return to France after his pardon.

17. Arthur Arnould (1837–1895)—Employee at the ministry of public instruction. Member of the International. Member of the Commune for the fourth arrondissement. Friend and ally of Bakunin while in exile. Embraced theosophy in his final years.

In my opinion the Commune should only meet to question the Committee of Public Safety concerning its acts or to judge a member of the Commune. This is what I said. It was a formal affirmation and not an incrimination of the consequences of Article 3. I ask that this fundamental rectification be made to the *Officiel*.

Citizen President: Rectification shall be made to the *Officiel*.

Citizen Arnould: I made a formal affirmation and not an incrimination of Article 3. The Commune should assist the Committee of Public Safety and if need be revoke it if it doesn't carry out its mandate, but it must stop discussing. We must meet in our arrondissements, follow our battalions when they march on the enemy, and avoid sterile discussions. I do not see in this either separation or hostility.

Citizen Paschal Grousset: You should have said this instead of publicly accusing us.

Citizen Arnould: We came here last Monday to explain ourselves, but there was no session. (Interruptions)

Citizen Régère: The publication of the separation signed by the minority is a regrettable act. But really, if that declaration went further than our colleagues' ideas, let them withdraw it. Their goal is the same as ours. We only differ on the means, and as soon as they return to us we should receive them fraternally so that we can all work together toward the goal we are pursuing. In any case, it was the minority that supported Citizen Lefrançais when he demanded that the broadest powers over the delegations be given to the Committee of Public Safety. (Noise)

It was the minority that wanted the latter to be able to strike the delegations. (Interruptions, noise)

A large number of voices: That isn't correct!

Citizen Régère: Come citizens; you have returned and you will remain among us.

Citizen Courbet:[18] But we are all here for the safety of the public.

---

18. Gustave Courbet (1819–1877)—One of the greatest of French painters. Member of the Commune for the sixth arrondissement. In charge of the demolition of the Vendôme Column, in payment for which his works were seized after the Commune. Sentenced to prison, he fled to Switzerland.

Citizen Jules Andrieux: It was said that the minority separated from the majority because it didn't want to accept a defeat in the election of the Committee of Public Safety. If that were correct then the minority would have been in the wrong. But this reproach is unfounded. The minority proposed its resolution because a motion was placed on the desk by the Committee of Public Safety, though everyone was in agreement that the Committee of Public Safety didn't have to consult us but rather should act. It seemed to us that there was only one thing to do, and that was to withdraw to our arrondissements and delegations as long as we weren't relieved. And I never participated more actively than I have since these events. I understood the economy of the proposal submitted by Citizen Miot. It was said that you would abdicate your authority as long as the Committee of Public Safety would meet. (Interruptions and prolonged noise)

Citizen Félix Pyat: I demand the reading of the minority's manifesto.

Citizen Jules Andrieu: Please allow me to finish. We didn't come to discuss. We came to tell you that the day when you will want a discussion we will explain everything, not to judges but to the Commune, without either passion or splits.

Several members: The motion!

Citizen Raoul Rigault: I requested the floor for a motion. The signers of the manifesto have declared that they will only present themselves to this assembly when the Commune will have set itself up as a court of justice. And so I don't understand either the presence of some of them among us or the discussion that is occurring at this moment. (Approbation)

Citizen Vaillant: On the question we are dealing with, I feel that I am so impartial that I can make observations that others here cannot make. I am a member of neither the majority nor the minority, since I was unable to find any group of men with whom I can march. Given what has happened, I ask that the assembly act like an assembly charged with saving Paris. We don't need internecine quarrels. This manifesto has delivered a serious blow to the Commune by placing before the public questions that should only be brought up in secret committee. But when these members, disavowing their manifesto, return here, we shouldn't wave it in their faces, forcing them to persevere in their error.

I spoke of the minority. But note this well, citizens: there was an act that provided if not the excuse, then at least the explanation for the error committed by several members of this assembly, and that was the change in the military commission. And so there is only one thing to do now: let the minority tear up its program and let the majority tell it: "Let's unite our efforts for the salvation of all. Be with us, for if you are against us we will smash you."

Citizen Billioray:[19] I will answer Citizen Vaillant by saying that we changed the military commission because that commission, charged with arresting Rossel, allowed him to escape. We couldn't keep men in place who didn't obey the orders of the Commune. If the members who signed the manifesto withdraw their signatures and tear up their declaration I think that the discussion on this question should be closed.

Citizen Amouroux: As concerns the manifesto, I will say that the members who signed it did great harm to the majority by seeking to make them look like parliamentarians. (Noise)

I declare that it was the majority that was the first to demand that there be only two sessions per week. The proof is that it was Citizens Delescluze, Vésinier, and Amouroux who made this proposal: Considering that all efforts should be focused on the war and the organization of the defense, the Commune decrees:

> Article 1. All members of the Commune shall be at the head of their arrondissements and legions.
> Article 2. The war commission will centralize all reports and will make them known at the sessions of the Commune.
> Article 3. The sessions of the Commune will take place on Sundays and Mondays at exactly 1:00 P.M.
> Article 4. The Commune can be convoked on an emergent basis upon the request of five members.

This proposal is dated May 5.

---

19. Alfred Billioray (1841–1877)—Artist. Member of the Commune and the Committee of Public Safety. Died in deportation in New Caledonia.

You cannot grant yourselves the monopoly of everything in your arrondissements and legions, because we revolutionaries are the ones who demanded it. You did everything, you attempted everything to become the majority, and when you saw that it escaped you abdicated through a manifesto in your papers.

We too ask to be in our arrondissements and on the ramparts, and it's for this reason that we named a Committee of Public Safety, so as to avoid sterile discussions. But far from abdicating, we asked for two sessions weekly to examine the conduct of the Committee and to reverse its decisions at its first error.

Citizen Frankel: I feel that I am in the same situation as my friend Vaillant. I don't belong to any fraction of the Commune, and yet I signed the conclusions of the manifesto and will defend it before you and my voters.

The Committee of Public Safety smashed the war commission because it included men who had voted against it. It surrounds itself with more or less capable men, as long as they go along with it. If the manifesto was published, it is your fault; we came here and you weren't here.

As long as you haven't relieved me, I will remain in my delegation and I will continue to concern myself with the interests of the workers, which I've done until now. I will send the decisions taken in accordance with the labor commission of the Committee of Public Safety. But I declare to you that I will only come here under the conditions indicated in the manifesto.

Citizen Urbain, the President: The minority should accept the actions of the Committee of Public Safety and not put stumbling blocks before it. In acting in this way it fails to do its duty. What is the minority going to do in its arrondissements? You only have one duty to fulfill, and that is that of withdrawing your manifesto and remaining here to watch over the safety of the revolution.

Citizen Viard:[20] In order to summarize and terminate the question, I request that the minority not only disavow its manifesto

---

20. Pompée Viard (1836–1892)—Paint merchant. Member of the Commune for the twentieth arrondissement. Delegate for subsistence and security. Sentenced to death in absentia. In exile grew close to the Blanquists and died an anarchist.

but also that it no longer put the Committee of Public Safety in question. It's doubtless because it is afraid that the minority acts as it does, but for my part I declare that the Committee of Public Safety cannot harm me and that it doesn't want to do so. In any case, don't we have the right to control it, and can't we strip it of power if need be? What we need more than anything is not only our devotion to the people's interests and our abnegation but also our political unity.

Citizen President: I will now give a reading of a first motion, signed by Vaillant: "The so-called declaration of the minority not having been directly produced in the Commune, and the presence of several members of that minority at today's session de facto annulling the declaration made by a portion of the assembly, the Commune passes to the motion."

This motion is not taken under consideration.

Here then is a second motion, signed by Miot: "Considering that the Committee of Public Safety is responsible for its acts, that it is at every moment at the orders and disposal of the Commune, whose sovereignty has never been nor could be contested, the majority of the Commune declares:

1. That it is ready to forget the conduct of those members of the minority who will withdraw their signature from the manifesto.

2. That it condemns the latter and passes to the motion."

Citizen Courbet: I request to make a motion. It is impossible for me to remain at the head of the town hall of my arrondissement. I am unable to obtain information from the delegation for war, especially since my municipal council has resigned.

Several voices: That's not a motion!

Citizen Courbet: Being responsible for my administration, I can no longer remain in this situation.

Several voices: That's not the question!

Citizen Serraillier:[21] I signed the manifesto while reserving to myself the right to come to the session. There is only one thing

---

21. Auguste Serraillier (1840–?)—Bootmaker. Member of the International. Member of the Commune for the second arrondissement. Member of the labor and exchange commission. Sentenced to death in absentia. Befriended

we can be attacked for, and that's the publicity that was given it. We came Sunday and Monday to participate in the session and there was no one. (Various calls) So we then wrote the manifesto and I will not renounce it. Doing so would be a culpable act. (The motion! Cloture!)

Citizen Langevin: I request the floor to speak against cloture. I have something personal that I want to speak about.

Citizens Victor Clément[22] and J.-B. Clément request the floor to speak against cloture.

Several members: To a vote! To a vote!

Citizen President: I put cloture to a vote.

Cloture is put to a vote and pronounced.

Citizen Langevin: Citizen Urbain said that the minority had supported Lefrançais's proposal, which conferred the Committee of Public Safety with plenary powers over the commissions and delegations. I am proud to have voted with the minority in many circumstances, but I reject Citizen Urbain's assertion. I voted against the Committee of Public Safety's motion, which gave it plenary powers.

Citizen Urbain, president: I maintain my assertion.

Citizen J.-B. Clément: I don't accept despotism, and I protest against the cloture vote. Conspiracies were spoken of and I want to defend myself. (Interruptions) We are told to run to our neglected municipalities; many among those of the minority have never gone to their town halls.

Citizen Dereure: That's true!

Citizen President: Cloture was voted and I must sustain it.

Citizen Ostyn:[23] You didn't sustain it when you let people speak.

---

by the Marx family while in exile; relations that ended after a financial disagreement with Marx's son-in-law Paul Lafargue.

22. Victor Clément (1824–?)—Mutualist. Member of the Commune for the fifteenth arrondissement. Sentenced to three years imprisonment for his role on the Commune.

23. Charles Ostyn (a.k.a. François Hosteins) (1823–1912)—Lathe operator. Member of the International. Member of the Commune for the nineteenth arrondissement. Sat on the subsistence and public services commissions. Sentenced to death in absentia. While in exile allied himself with the

Citizen J.-B. Clément: I ask to respond as well.

Citizen Régère: I request that we vote on the motion of Citizen Vaillant. This motion, all of whose terms I don't accept—since I believe Citizen Vaillant has gone beyond his ideas—nevertheless gives satisfaction to the majority and the main interests of the Commune, because it states that the minority, by resuming its seats here, tacitly disavows its regrettable manifesto.

Citizen President: I gave readings of the two motions put forth by Citizens Miot and Vaillant. I am going to put them to a vote.

Citizen Victor Clément: I will not vote. Given that I don't recognize a majority's right to commit a minority, I don't recognize our right to commit our colleagues.

Citizen Pyat: You declared that the Commune had abdicated.

Citizen Victor Clément: Will Citizen Pyat permit me to speak only of the motion? I think that if there is someone who has never stirred up passions in a debate, it is I.

Citizen J. Miot pronounces a few words that don't reach us.

Citizen Victor Clément: I will answer Citizen Miot by saying that if he wants to descend to the realm of intentions we'll never finish. For my part, I would never insult a member of the Commune by believing that outside his acts he has evil intentions. It's your right to condemn our manifesto, but what I call for is an act of justice. We can't vote the motion because that would mean committing colleagues who are not here.

Citizen Arnould: In response to an interruption, I will say that if I wasn't at my town hall it's because I had an important delegation that took up my time.

Citizen Dereure: You had no need to say that the municipal administrations were neglected.

Citizen President: I put to a vote the two motions that have been proposed.

The motion proposed by Citizen Vaillant is voted on and rejected. The motion proposed by Citizen Miot is then put to a vote and adopted.

---

anarchists. In 1971 his hometown of Colombes renamed the Rue Thiers the Rue Ostyn.

Citizen Billioray (returning): The cartridge depot on the Rue Rapp has just exploded and it's still burning. This is treason and yet you talk! They've arrested the traitor who set the fire. (Movement)

Citizen President: I will no longer cede the floor on the question of the manifesto.

Citizen Vaillant: I ask the members who are in charge of the municipalities to please listen to me. The Commune gave me a delegation in which I often find myself in conflict with certain municipalities, while with others everything is for the best. Education doesn't function as it should. Today I will speak to you about the Jesuits. They are intervening everywhere and in every way. The enthusiastic municipalities were done with them in two days; in others they weren't able to be driven out. It is urgent that two months after March 18 we should see no more of these people. It would be good if the municipalities were to be a bit more zealous . . .

Citizen Régère: Be precise!

Citizen Vaillant: . . . and make them completely disappear within forty-eight hours. Here is what I propose: "On the proposal of the delegation for education the Commune decides: Given the many warnings given to the arrondissement municipalities to substitute secular education for religious education;

Within forty-eight hours a list shall be compiled of all the schools still held by the congregations. This list shall be published every day in the *Officiel*, including the names of the members of the Commune delegated to the municipal government of the arrondissement where the orders of the Commune on the subject of the establishment of strictly secular education have nor been executed."

Citizen Vaillant's proposal, put to a vote, is adopted.

Citizen Ostyn: I request that I be allowed to place on the desk the list of the religious communities that exist within Paris.

Citizen Mortier:[24] I have an important question to address. A police superintendent came to our arrondissement to evacuate

---

24. Henri Mortier (1843–1894)—Jigsaw operator. Blanquist. Member of the International. Member of the Commune for the eleventh arrondissement. Presided over committee for pensions and indemnities of widows and

and close the church. This operation was carried out in such a way that it caused a riot in the neighborhood. Why weren't we notified in advance?

Citizen Courbet: In the presence of serious acts that are occurring at various points General Safety had to take exceptional measure and execute them without delay. It believes it has done its duty. (Yes!)

Citizen Gambon:[25] At a time like this we should exclusively concern ourselves with the war and all the questions that go with it. (Agreement)

Citizen Urbain, president: Citizen Vésinier[26] proposes the following decrees:

1. Titles of nobility, coats of arms, liveries, noble privileges and honorific distinctions are abolished. Pensions, rents, prerogatives, and all that go along with these are suppressed.
2. Increases of all kinds are abolished, and the rents, pensions, and privileges that flow from them are suppressed.
3. The Legion of Honor and all honorific orders are abolished. A subsequent decree will determine which legionnaire pensions should be maintained; the rest shall be suppressed.

Another proposal:

The law of May 8, 1816, is annulled. The decree of March 21, 1803, promulgated the 31st of that month is once again in effect.

All recognized children are legitimate and will enjoy all the rights of legitimate children.

---

orphans. Sentenced to death in absentia. Lived most of his remaining years in exile, continuing his Blanquist activities.

25. Ferdinand Gambon (1820–1887)—Lawyer and magistrate. People's representative in 1848 in the Jacobin faction. Member of the Commune, elected by the tenth arrondissement. Fought until the final moments of the Commune and fled to Switzerland, where he joined the International.

26. Pierre Vésinier (1824–1902)—Journalist. Member of the International. Member of the Commune for the first arrondissement. Editor in chief of *Paris Libre* and directed the *Journal Officiel* during the Commune's final weeks. Sentenced to death in absentia. Described by a contemporary as "one of the least sympathetic personalities of the Commune."

All so-called natural children who are not recognized are recognized by the Commune as legitimate.

All male citizens aged eighteen and female citizens aged sixteen who declare before a municipal magistrate that they want to unite in the ties of marriage shall be united, on the condition that they also declare that they are not married and that they have neither father nor mother nor relatives up to the degree that in the eyes of the law is a hindrance to marriage.

They are dispensed from any other legal formality.

Their children, if they have any, will be recognized as legitimate on their simple declaration.

And another proposal of Citizen Durand's:

I propose to the Commune that it decree that in the future no move can take place until a customs officer or some other agent of the Commune has checked the packaging.

Citizen J.-B. Clément's proposal is put to a vote and urgently adopted.

Citizen President: Here is a proposal made by Citizen Miot: "I ask the justice commission if it is ready to make its report on my proposal relating to the reform of the prisons."

Upon the request of Citizen Ledroit a reading is given of the following proposal, made by the council of the Fifth Legion:

Considering that every honest citizen has the right to fight for his country's freedom in whatever camp chance has placed him,

Decrees:

Article 1. Any citizen who will have taken part in the defense of communal freedoms and the republic will have the right to a pension of 300 francs, the first quarterly amount of which will be paid three months after the day when total victory is carried off by the defenders of the republic over the Versaillais royalists.

Article 2. Any soldier from the Versaillais army, whatever corps he may belong to, who lines up under the banner of the Commune and the republic will have the right to the same pension.

Article 3. Any citizen from the provinces who takes up arms to defend the republic and the communal institutions will also have a right to the same pension.

Article 4. Any officer or non-commissioned officer of the Versailles army who comes to defend the flag of freedom will have right to a pension in proportion to his rank.

Citizen Billioray: I request that I be allowed to read you a dispatch that I just received on the subject of the explosion that just occurred on the Avenue Rapp. (Movement of lively interest)

A reading of the dispatch is made.

Citizen President: In the face of all that is happening we should show less hesitation in voting for the repressive measures that are proposed to us. (Yes)

A member: I ask that a war contribution be voted against the shopkeepers who left Paris to escape service in the National Guard. (Supported)

Citizen President: This proposal will be discussed at a later time. Citizens, I inform you that our next session will be the day after tomorrow.

Citizen Léo Frankel: Given the events that are currently taking place I declare that I will participate in the sessions.

Citizen President: The minutes will state that Citizen Léo Frankel has withdrawn his signature from the manifesto.

The session is adjourned at 7:00 P.M.

The secretaries,
Amouroux, Vésinier

■ INQUIRY ON THE COMMUNE

In 1897 *La Revue Blanche*, one of France's most important and influential literary journals, ran an "Inquiry on the Commune" in two of its issues asking participants the following three questions:

1. What was your role from March 18 to the end of May 1871?

2. What is your opinion of the insurrectionary movement of the Commune, and what do you think of its parliamentary, military, financial, and administrative organization?

3. In your opinion, what has been the influence of the Commune, both then and now, on events and ideas?

The following are chosen from among the dozens of participants.

HENRI ROCHEFORT[1]

Q: *What was your role during the Commune?*
A: I simply did my duty as a journalist. I didn't take part in the Commune. But since I clearly published my opinion of Versailles, whose conduct I found odious, I was accused of provoking the rebellion.

Q: *On March 18?*
A: No, later. On March 18 I was in Arcachon, so ill that my death was announced. In Arcachon I received a visit from my children, who were dressed in mourning for their father.

Q: *You arrived in Paris?*
A: April 2, the day, I think, of Flourens's sortie. *Le Mot d'Ordre*, which I was writing for, was suppressed by Ladmirault, that old, vile brute.

Q: *Can we do without the epithets?*
A: No. Ladmirault was an ignoble brute, as were all the professional soldiers. I ignored the prohibition. The government had slipped away to Versailles. I energetically supported Paris's rights. I spoke of Thiers's odious role and his abominable lies. Naturally, all of my sympathies were with the Communal movement, which was both socialist and patriotic. The Commune was a protest against the peace of Bordeaux, a protest against the clerical and reactionary majority that dishonored us, a protest against the abuse of power of an assembly which, named to negotiate peace, had—without a mandate—declared itself constituent. But the Commune became authoritarian and suppressed the newspapers that weren't devoted to it. Raoul Rigault and Félix Pyat suppressed newspapers; Felix Pyat in particular suppressed newspapers for his own profit. I fought for freedom and good sense, as I did all

---

1. Henri Rochefort (1831–1913)—Indefatigable propagandist. Exiled under Napoleon III for his writings in *La Lanterne*, upon returning to France he led Victor Noir's funeral cortège. Refused to be a candidate for the Commune. Arrested by the Prussians he was sentenced by the Versaillais to deportation, from which he escaped. Main propagandist for the Boulangist movement, and later a virulent anti-Semite and opponent of Dreyfus.

my life. Raoul Rigault suppressed *Le Mot d'Ordre*. The pretext was my protest against the hostage decree, or rather its execution. We followed the example given by our African generals who, in the name of the government, had taken hostages there and massacred them. Those who had applauded the massacres and razzias in Africa found the Commune's conduct odious. I found it natural, but I didn't want the decree executed. It was this article that later led to me being placed before a military tribunal by the Versaillais. Idiocy! Idiocy! Always the soldiers! All imbeciles. Do you know what they held against me? It's that in the headline the word "hostages" was typed in capital letters. It's idiotic. I approved the decree and I protested against its execution. Raoul Rigault wanted to have me arrested. I was warned of this by a young man, a secretary of Rigault's I think.

Q: *Forain?*
A: No, not Forain, a member of the Commune's police. I left. I was arrested in Meaux on the twenty-first.

Q: *Was there an order against you from the Versaillais?*
A: Not at all; it was from Raoul Rigault. He was an excellent man, quite intelligent. All right. But he was for the fight to the finish. He knew what the Versaillais would do, and he was right. He took no extenuating circumstances into consideration. No quarter! He had participated in my newspaper, but he was a man who would have executed his best friend. If I had been seized by the Commune there was no question what would have happened to me. But in Meaux I was taken by the Versaillais. The commander of the German subdivision wanted to allow me to leave; I remained in prison despite the Prussians. At the court-martial those brutes took no account of what I had to say. I was on the point of being executed; it was a near thing. Perhaps what saved me was Rossel's arrest, which occurred at just that moment. He went ahead of me. The court-martial had already sentenced members of the Commune to death; it condemned Rossel to death. Perhaps they decided to take it easy on me. I spent five months in prison. After a two-day trial I was sentenced to deportation for life, which in civil matters is equivalent to the death penalty. Even worse, we were dealing with such ignorant judges that they didn't even know that

the death penalty in political matters had been abolished since 1848. Officers! I remember that in prison I was Rossel's neighbor. I had won over our guard by sharing with him the victuals that were sent to me; he let us talk. I owe him the few good hours that I passed with the unfortunate Rossel, who they didn't sentence to death but who they assassinated. Note that before '48 the law punished soldiers who revolted or went over to the enemy with death. Since then the only ones punished with death were traitors: it is by virtue of this law that they killed Rossel. (M. Da Costa, who was present for the interview, observed that of three officers tried and judged by the government of the Third Republic, Rossel, Bazaine, and Dreyfus, only one was sentenced to death: Rossel.)

Rossel was assassinated. I was sentenced to deportation for life to a fortified place as leader of a gang and for inciting to revolt. Jules Simon later told me that Thiers had done all in his power to prevent me from being executed. Cissey the thief, the swindler who poisoned himself, Cissey the general, the minister of war, the supporter of Order and Religion, Cissey demanded that I be executed. In the name of the army he demanded my execution. Thiers defended me. He carried on. He cried. He said that they couldn't put to death a former member of the government. If they executed members of the government . . . he . . . But the fact is, it appears he cried in my behalf. He didn't even want me deported. In the end he agreed that I be imprisoned on an island outside of France. There are no islands that aren't outside France. But in the prison prepared for me on Saint-Marguerite, Bazaine was also imprisoned. Edmond Adam showed me a letter from the director of that prison, telling him he wouldn't be a severe host in my regard but that I would have to do picket duty. You understand that I didn't want any kind of exceptional treatment, and I feared being a prisoner who was, so to speak, on parole. I was already thinking of escaping. In the midst of all this, on May 24 Thiers was overthrown and I was deported. It's pointless, isn't it, to tell you how I escaped, with Jourde, Olivier Pain, Paschal Grousset, Ballière, Granthille; how I lived in London, in Geneva, and finally my return . . .

Q: *Your triumphal return. And your opinion of the Commune?*

A: As the Empire had fallen, we believed in the republic. When we ended up with an Assembly even more clerical and reactionary than the preceding ones, we revolted. The majority had exasperated me, and that's why I tendered my resignation in Bordeaux. The Parisians had had enough. The Commune was the explosion of duped and betrayed republican sentiments. Thiers admitted it: the insurrection was produced by the exasperation of disappointed patriotism. Governments rarely change, and they continue to exasperate the governed.

(Going on to talk about Greece, M. Rochefort shows us a statuette that the Greeks just sent him, and ingeniously explains to us what a Tanagra is.)

Q: *But the Commune, your opinion?*
A: The Commune, quite simply, is the only honest government there has been in France since Pharamond. The rulers earned fifteen francs a day. Since then they cost us a bit more. I was with them when I was deported. Not a single one of these men had a sou.

Q: *But these honest men, do you think that they were able, were well inspired?*
A: It depends. There were moderates and extremists. Naturally, it was the extremists who were right. When you want to act you can't take half measures, or else . . . Look, the Greeks are hardly anything compared to France, but if they remain boastful up to the bitter end, they'll likely win out over all the powers.

Q: *The administration?*
A: I know very little about it.

Q: *And the influence of the Commune?*
A: Enormous. The massacres by the Versaillais have forever discredited bourgeois society. And then the Commune saved the republic.

Q: *That we have.*
A: I don't want to say anything. Nevertheless, it remains the example.

PASCHAL GROUSSET[2]

Member of the Commune, during the Commune, delegate for external relations, currently deputy

It's not only a chapter of my life story that you are asking about, it's a whole volume. The volume is written but will only come out after my death. Let it sleep. In a few words, here are my feelings about March 18.

It's hardly necessary to affirm that two million men don't rise up without reason, don't fight for nine weeks and don't leave thirty-five thousand corpses on the streets without having good reasons.

For many, these reasons were the result of the long suffering which is the life of seven eighths of a so-called civilized nation. For others they were principally born of anger born of the siege, of a great effort made sterile through official incompetence, of the shame of the capitulation, and also by an agreement made easier by the coming together of civic forces. For most people the dominant idea, the main idea, was the primordial need to defend the republic, directly attacked by a clerical and royalist Assembly.

The republic of our dreams was assuredly not the one we have. We wanted it to be democratic and social, not plutocratic. We wanted to make it a precision instrument of economic transformation. For us, republic was synonymous with regeneration. Amid the smoking ruins of the fatherland it seemed to us necessary and right to completely disqualify the men and institutions who had caused these ruins. We needed new schools, a new morality, and new guides. Work for all, education for all, national defense for all, unshakeable confidence in the destiny of our race: these were the slogans that spontaneously rose from the heart of a bloodied Paris and which in its eyes was embodied by the republic.

---

2. Paschal Grousset (1844–1893)—Journalist, opponent of the Bonapartist regime. Victor Noir was murdered while acting as Grousset's second in a duel with Pierre Bonaparte, setting off massive anti-government demonstrations. Member of the Commune for the eighteenth arrondissement. Member of the external affairs commission. Sentenced to deportation to New Caledonia. Escaped along with Henri Rochefort and Francis Jourde. Later an independent socialist deputy.

The siege left us militarily organized; this is why our revolution was both military and civil. The ruling classes had just given the measure of their criminal incapacity. This is why our revolution was proletarian and marks the pivotal fact of modern times, which is the direct access of the workers to the mysteries of power.

As for the Commune, for us as for those of 1792, it was the chance and provisional organism that is born at moments of crisis to take social evolution in hand and to lead it to its goal.

You already know how the struggle was engaged and what its course was. Thanks to the complicity of Germany, which purposely turned its three hundred thousand prisoners over to the Assembly at Versailles, Paris fell before numbers. But at least, by its heroic effort it gave republican France the time to take itself in hand. Formal commitments were made by Thiers with the delegates of the major, frightened cities. When the blood was washed from our streets it was discovered that Paris's program was the only practical one.

It is thus that from our holocaust, from our pain, from the tears of our mothers, that the republican pact was solidified. In the meanwhile, the municipal law was voted. On this point as well Paris won the day.

As for the economic transformation, it was put off for a quarter century. But who today would dare to say that it has not remained inevitable? Poverty grows along with mechanical progress. In this beautiful France, thousands of arms have nothing to do. The malaise of every class is betrayed by symptoms that are more obvious with each passing day. The impotence of old formulas, the incoherence of institutions and acts is clear for all to see. The hour is approaching when on this point too the program of March 18 will impose itself by the force of circumstances. For we who wanted to advance it this hour will be that of historic justice.

ÉDOUARD VAILLANT[3]

Member of the Commune, currently deputy

Without being as clear about it as I am now, I was nevertheless convinced from the beginning of the revolution of March 18, that there should be only one dominant preoccupation and goal: the fight against Versailles. To be or not to be—for the Commune that was the whole question. The facts, the circumstances had posed things in this way. If not to win, it had at least to last. However important it was to make manifest its revolutionary socialist character by all possible acts, nothing could better affirm this character than its very existence, its resistance. It was that and the rage, the fury of capitalism's reaction; the coalesced efforts against Paris of Versailles and Bismarck.

Those who during the siege had participated in the agitation, in the revolutionary socialist action concentrated at the Corderie, seat of the Committee of the Twenty Arrondissements and who, at the cry of "Vive la Commune!" had attacked the Hôtel de Ville on October 8, penetrated it on October 31, and on January 22 had attempted, for the defense of the republic and for the revolution, to seize power, these people were not in a state of uncertainty. Throughout the siege they had seen the revolutionary movement grow, though it didn't attract the populace, duped by the lies and charlatanry of its rulers. They were able to foresee the popular anger and revolt on the day of disillusionment and open betrayal. And this is indeed what happened when, after having responded to our red poster that it wouldn't capitulate, the government capitulated and from hatred of the revolution, surrendered Paris and the country to the monarchic invader, which had become its counter-revolutionary ally.

Events had dispersed the committee of the Corderie and the arrondissement committees. Their most active members had made the mistake of going into the provinces, to such a point that

---

3. Édouard Vaillant (1840–1915)—Engineer. Blanquist. Member of the International. Member of the Commune for the eighth arrondissement. Member of the executive commission. Proposed worker control of abandoned workshops and oversaw the reopening of Paris's museums. Fought on the barricades till the final moments. Sentenced to death in absentia. In London became a friend and ally of Marx in the fight with Bakunin.

they weren't at the head of the tumultuously growing movement that followed the governmental betrayal, where all the angered and rebellious currents of opinion would finally mix together.

The Central Committee of the National Guard was the expression of that uncertain and intermediary period, from which came, with the March 26 election, the elected Commune.

Several revolutionaries from the Corderie and revolutionaries and socialists from various groups entered the Commune. And so this election gave it a momentum, a direction, that was more socialist. The elected Commune was far from being what the committee of the Corderie would have been, the revolutionary Commune, master of power. It had neither that unity of ideas and action nor that energy. It was a deliberative assembly without sufficient cohesion, whose decisiveness wasn't on a par with its good will and intentions. What we can say in praise of it is that it was truly the representative, the socialist representative of Paris in revolt, and it did its best to represent it and defend it.

We can also add that most of the citizens who were delegates there did honor to their mandates. And we must pay honors less to them than to the revolutionary and enthusiastic environment that lifted everything up and made it grow. It was an environment that in those unforgettable and admirable weeks, made of the people of Paris in arms—at first to guard its weapons against reaction and the provocations of Versailles, and then increasingly for working-class emancipation and the revolution—a people of combatants and citizens.

And in fact, as the threat of defeat became more pressing, the revolutionary spirit increasingly animated those who remained standing, those who lived, who fought. They truly represented Paris and its people. It is their fight and their death that constituted their grandeur in the eyes of the world, made all the greater by the ferocity of those who carried out the massacres: the grandeur of the Paris Commune.

When for many days Paris was isolated, in flames, slaughtered by the Versaillais assassins, was dying, in the eyes of all it became the incarnation of the proletariat fighting for its deliverance and the revolution militant. The prolonged fury of Versaillais reaction, applauded and assisted by the reaction and capitalism of all countries, spread this impression everywhere, confirmed this effect, gave more éclat to this calling to life of the organized revolt of all the poor, of all the oppressed.

And so the struggle and the fall of the Commune, its history and legend, were the universal evocation of socialist and revolutionary consciousness. And in those countries where there had until then only been democratic demands, socialism was affirmed. If socialism wasn't born of the Commune, it is from the Commune that dates that portion of international revolution that no longer wants to give battle in a city in order to be surrounded and crushed but which instead wants, at the head of the proletarians of each and every country, to attack national and international reaction and put an end to the capitalist regime.

M. PINDY[4]
Member of the Commune

What do I think of the insurrection, of its organization? I think we acted like children who try to imitate grownups whose names and reputations subjugate them, and not like men with force (at least a certain force) should have done in the face of the eternal enemy. I am far from being a passionate admirer of what we did during the Commune, and I think that aside from a minority of our colleagues whose time at the Hôtel de Ville gave them the idea that they were statesmen, the others, and the people along with them, have become convinced that the best of governments is worth nothing and that authority, in whatever hands it is placed, is always harmful to the advancement of humanity.

Le Chaux-de-Fonds

4. Jean-Louis Pindy (1840–1917)—Carpenter. Member of the International. Member of the Commune for the third arrondissement. Ordered the fire at the Hôtel de Ville. Sentenced to death in absentia. Lived in Switzerland and was an active anarchist.

M. DEREURE[5]
Cobbler

Elected in November 1870 to the municipality of the eighteenth arrondissement with Clemenceau, Lafont, and Jaclard, I remained at my fighting post, faithful to the insurrection. Elected a member of the Commune on March 26, I fought for its cause until the final day of combat.

Q: *The parliamentary organization?*
A: The Commune concerned itself far too much with details it would have been preferable to look after only after the military victory. It was powerfully organized. The Central Committee of the National Guard, which had been elected to prevent the Prussians from entering Paris and which met March 18 at the Hôtel de Ville, didn't understand its role and didn't want to take the responsibility for throwing its battalions at Versailles from the beginning. It left Thiers the time to organize the besieging army and it only worried about the elections to the Commune. Nevertheless, it had taken measures to seize the forts, but it sent the absinthe addict Lullier to Mont-Valérien; I had to shake Lullier, dead drunk, on a couch in the Hôtel de Ville. And based on the illusory promise of the fort's commander, the traitor didn't leave there the battalions he had brought. And after the sortie of April 3, a sortie that had been organized by some members of the Commune without the consent of the latter, the Parisians were stupefied and immediately demoralized at finding themselves under fire from Mont-Valérien. Confidence was lost. I estimate that after this defeat there weren't forty thousand men in rotation who defended Paris. I was often at the forward position, and the constant request of the superior officers was, "We are lacking men; we need reinforcements." Toward the end of the Commune I was delegated to Dombrowski to keep an eye on his actions. Versailles had offered him a million to withdraw his forces from one of the

---

5. Simon Dereure (1838–1900)—Cobbler. Member of the International. Member of the Commune for the eighteenth arrondissement. Sentenced to death in absentia. After a period in exile in New York joined the utopian community in Corning, Iowa.

gates; he had himself denounced this fact to the Committee of Public Safety. Did he betray? This is a point difficult to elucidate. I am convinced that he was not a traitor. What I saw was that it was absolutely impossible to send companies to the Point du Jour. The cannons of Mont-Valérien, of Montretout, and the heights of Issy rained down on it. Something interesting is that the chateau of La Muette, where the general staff was located, only received two cannon shots, one on the staircase and one in the stable. Placed as it was—within range of the cannons of Mont-Valérien—it should have been pulverized. There must have been two or three informants on the general staff whose lives had to be preserved.

Q: *Financially?*
A: If the Commune would have placed an embargo on the Bank [of France] everything would have worked much better, and it's not just a question of that Bank but of all the banks. And they should have also seized the daily receipts of all the railroad companies. A detail: I remember seeing the directors of these companies at the ministry of Finance, where Varlin had invited them. They were across from two workers, Varlin, a bookbinder, and me, a cobbler. And these people who are said to be so arrogant, showed such obsequiousness that I'm still disgusted by it.

Q: *Administratively?*
A: All services were easily reorganized and functioned with no difficulty.

Q: *What do you think of the role of the Central Committee after the elections to the Commune?*
A: There was a harmful duality, but it was impossible for the Commune to smash the Central Committee, which had the National Guard in its hands.

Q: *Did you have the illusion that you could emerge victors?*
A: We had no illusions. And in general the members of the Commune sacrificed their lives. But with regard to the masses, we didn't think the repression would be so ignobly cruel.

Q: *Once the Versaillais were in Paris, do you think that all the members of the Commune did their duty?*

A: No, it seems that the primary concern of some among them was to hide. In the final hours I recall seeing Ranvier, Varlin, Ferré, Gambon, Theisz, Jourde, Serraillier, and Trinquet. Others were fighting at other points; others had been taken prisoner or had been blocked in their neighborhoods. Durand, Rigault, and Varlin were executed. Delescluze died at the barricades. Others were wounded: Vermorel, Arnaud, Protot, and Brunel. If, many were able to escape once the battle was finished, it's because the Empire's police had been totally disorganized.

Q: *And the barricades?*
A: The barricades were good, but we didn't make enough use of houses. The Versaillais, on the contrary, knew how to use them. In the final days, the best defenders of the Commune were unquestionably the children and the elderly.

JEAN ALLEMANE[6]

Editor-in-chief of the Parti Ouvrier

March 18, 1871, was a day that was wished for and prepared by M. Thiers and his accomplices, determined to have done with the popular National Guard (the armed workers), in the same way that their kin of the provisional government of 1848 put an end to the workers of the national workshops.

The mistake these rotters committed was, in the first case, that of unmasking themselves by assisting the Bank of France in ruining hundreds of small merchants and factory owners by deciding the cessation of the deferral of commercial payments. This could very well have had serious consequences if, instead of well-intentioned citizens and unknowing socialists, the Central Committee had been composed of determined men capable of

---

6. Jean Allemane (1843–1920)—Republican under the Empire and active as an administrator under the Commune. Deported to New Caledonia for his activities, he returned and was an important figure in French socialism in later years, serving as a deputy.

guiding affairs by beginning their attack at the true center of resistance: the Bank of France. The members of the middle class, who were already overexcited by the patriotic disappointment, would have applauded the most daring measures.

Had determined men been in power during the insurrection, Messieurs Thiers and de Ploeuc, authorized representatives of the upper bourgeoisie and high finance, would have nothing left to do but say their mea culpa for having unleashed the hurricane. But the members of the Central Committee—as was later the case with those of the Commune—were motivated strictly by sentiments. Their lack of resolution, compounded by economic ignorance, made them lose the benefits of an exceptionally favorable situation, since in the eyes of all concerned the government's attack had taken on the character of a monarchical restoration. This led sincere republicans to avoid placing any obstacles before measures that were clearly socialist and revolutionary.

The main thing was to move quickly, and this was precisely what wasn't done.

Proclamations, more proclamations, and still more proclamations. During this time the reactionary beast recovered from the turmoil caused by the unforeseen resistance and the incidents of the war. This resistance caused the finest flower of the canaille to scurry to Versailles and, assisted by all the cowardice and all the parasitism that was being held at bay, the reactionary beast prepared its revenge. A revenge which history will recognize was at the same high level as the braggarts that the flat-footed Maxime Du Camp called "the party of honest men."

March 18, 1871, was willed by its leaders and could have marked the epoch of a new world for the despoiled. But in order to do this, instead of chattering, it should have struck the bourgeoisie at its most sensitive point: the safe!

That done, all that would have had to be left was to use the gold to disorganize the Versaillais gangs, something much easier to do in Paris than should have been. Had they been deprived of their gold then steel, resolutely employed, would have put an end to capitalist resistance.

Too "48-er" to consider this, the men of the Central Committee unconsciously repaired the errors committed by M. Thiers and his accomplices, and allowed them to prepare the murders of the Bloody Week.

JEAN GRAVE[7]

Editor of Les Temps Nouveaux, *who took no part in the Commune but whose opinion seemed of interest to us, the opinion of a revolutionary of today on the revolutionaries of the past.*

What I think of the parliamentary, financial, military, and administrative organization of the Commune can be summed up in just a few words.

It was too parliamentary, financial, military, and administrative and not revolutionary enough.

To start with, while every day the battalions of Federals gathered at their meeting places waiting for the order to march on Versailles, a movement whose urgency was clear to all, the Central Committee, on the pretext that it didn't have regular power, thought only of organizing elections, while the army of order was reforming in Versailles.

The Commune, once elected, busied itself with passing laws and decrees, most of which were not implemented, because those they were aimed at realized that the Commune legislated much but acted little.

Revolutionaries! That's nevertheless what they thought they were, but only in words and parades. So little were they really revolutionaries that even invested with the suffrage of the Parisians they continued to consider themselves intruders in the halls of power.

They lacked money, when hundreds of millions slept in the Bank of France. All they would have needed to do would have been to send out against the bank two or three battalions of

---

7. Jean Grave (1854–1939)—One of the central figures of French anarchism in the period after the Commune. Editor for *Le Révolté*, *La Révolte*, and *Les Temps Nouveaux*.

National Guardsmen to have the Marquis de Ploeuc—who so easily fooled them—go flee into the shadows.

They voted the law on hostages and never dared implement it, while Versailles continued to massacre the Federals who fell into their hands.

I'm not saying that it should have executed the handful of gendarmes and obscure priests it had in its hands. Versailles could have not have cared less: the serious hostages were out of the Commune's reach. But it had the survey records, the mortgage office, the notary records, everything that regulates bourgeois property. If instead of making threats the Commune had actually set all the paperwork on fire, had taken control of the bank, the same bourgeois who insulted the imprisoned Federals would have forced Thiers to apologize to them on their behalf.

In a revolution, legality is not only a joke but a hindrance; it can only serve the partisans of the order of affairs we want to destroy. It's not speeches, paperwork, or laws that are needed during a revolutionary period but acts.

Instead of voting for the forfeiture of bosses in flight, they should immediately have placed their workshops in the possession of the workers, who would have put them in operation. And it was the same for everything. Instead of laws and decrees that would have remained dead letters, they needed facts. Then they would have been taken seriously.

They wanted to play at being soldiers, to parade in the uniforms of Jacobin officers, as if revolutionaries had to make a disciplined war.

Attacked by the government of Versailles, they should have contented themselves with defending themselves. But they should only have given up ground foot by foot; they should have sapped terrain and houses so that every forward step of the soldiers of order would have been the equivalent of a defeat for them.

No, even backed against the wall in Paris they still wanted to develop strategy. They put up enormous barricades which, aimed to confront a designated point, were turned by the enemy. Impregnable head on, they left their defenders wide open from behind. It would have been so easy to crenellate houses, to make each of them a fortress and only abandon them after having set them on fire or blown them up. The Commune respected property! Versailles, its defender, was less scrupulous and didn't hesitate to destroy houses when they had to turn a barricade.

Now, it must be said that the men of the Commune aren't responsible for what wasn't done. They were of their period, and in their time if there was a vague socialist sentiment, no one, neither leaders nor soldiers, had clearly defined ideas. So it was inevitable that everyone end up mired in uncertainty.

Triumphant, the Commune would have become a government like the others. A new revolution would have been needed to bring it down. Vanquished, it synthesized all proletarian aspirations, and gave momentum to the movement of ideas of which we of today are the product.

LOUISE MICHEL[8]

For twenty-six years they've spoken of the victims of the Commune, about sixty whose names are known. The Commune's dead can't be counted. Paris was an immense abattoir where, after eight days of slaughter, the hordes of flies over the mass graves put an end to the killings for they feared the plague.

The number of dead of the Commune during the Bloody Week can't be calculated. They were buried everywhere, in the public squares, under the paving stones, in wells, in trenches dug at the time of the Prussians, in cemeteries, in casemates where they were burned. They were brought in wagons to the Champ de Mars, where they were also burned. The ashes weren't gathered and placed in urns; the winds that carried them away will tell neither their name nor their number.

---

8. Louise Michel (1830–1905)—Central figure of French anarchism. Held no position on the Commune but fought actively at the barricades. Deported to New Caledonia, she never ceased her anarchist activities. A historian of the Commune wrote of her, "She was always adored by those who knew her, esteemed by those she fought, venerated by those who esteemed her big heart and admired her valor."

And so the Commune, which naïvely waited for Versailles's attack and didn't plunge a spike in the stone heart of the vampire, the Bank of France, expiated its generosity.

But unvanquished under the avenging flames of the fire, it will be reborn even stronger, for it understood how useless political changes are that put one set of men in place of another set of men. It knew that the old parliamentary world would only ever produce what it produced on September 4, and this world has proved it since. Every revolution will now be social and not political; this was the final breath, the supreme aspiration of the Commune in the ferocious grandeur of its marriage with death.

The armies of the Commune counted few men knowledgeable in what is called the art of war, but all were equally brave. Cluseret, La Cécilia, Dombrowski, and Rossel were almost the only generals who came from the army, but enthusiasm and contempt for death have great value when the number of combatants is relatively small. This number was sometimes so small, as at Ivry, Clamart, and Neuilly, that it was an extraordinary stroke of luck that the enemy didn't know it. With combatants of this kind the Commune should have carried the situation from the first minutes. Already defeated, the Federal swarm for eight days halted the most formidable army that the Third Republic deployed.

It wasn't the moment for parliamentarism, and the Commune had no reason to praise the sessions it was engaged in, though it counted in its number eloquent men, like old Pyat, Vallès, and so many others. Majority and minority found themselves united at the final hour in the grandeur of same sacrifice.

You ask me, dear comrades, what my role was from March 18 to the end of May 1871. I went out with the marching companies of the Commune from the first sortie, I was a member of the Montmartre battalion, and I fought in the ranks as a soldier. In all conscience I thought this was the most useful thing to do. I continued fighting in Paris like the others, until Versailles arrested my mother in order to execute her in my place. I went to set her free (despite herself) by demanding that place for myself.

Many times I have told how during the voyage to Caledonia I became an anarchist. But when people started to talk about the Commune again and question us, it seemed to me that the events of that period were as if a thousand years from us, we who are like shadows, having passed through so many of the dead. Has the moment arrived when the specter of evil will be lifted?

London

JEAN-BAPTISTE CLÉMENT[9]
Member of the Commune

J.-B. Clément spoke to us about the frame of mind of his colleagues of the Commune.

Men like Theisz, Varlin, and Avrial[10] went no further than mutualism. Vermorel was an enemy of communism. But was there even a question of communism? The Blanquists, especially Vaillant, had the best feeling for the situation and often sounded the right note.

Q: *At the Commune you busied yourselves with decrees on payments due, on rents, on the municipal pawnshop.*
A: The debts due! How much talk has there been about this! I said, "Does this have anything to do with the Commune? Then let merchants make arrangements among themselves." As for the setting aside of the rents, it was not without difficulty that the

---

9. Jean-Baptiste Clément (1836–1903)—Writer. Elected to the Commune for the eighteenth arrondissement. Served on numerous commissions of the Commune. Tireless socialist militant until his death. Author of the song "Le Temps des Cerises." Buried near the Mur des Fédérés at Père Lachaise Cemetery.
10. Augustin Avrial (1840–1904)—Mechanic. Member of the International. Member of the Commune, representing the eleventh arrondissement. Distinguished himself on the barricades during the Bloody Week. Sentenced to death in absentia. Patented a sewing machine of his invention in 1892. Socialist militant until his death.

Commune voted it. And yet Paris was a barracks, and in a barracks they don't go so far as to make you pay rent.

At one session, having said, "Citizens, I thought we were here to proceed to social liquidation," Jourde[11] heckled me. Since I got angry, Ostyn calmed me down, while Varlin approved Jourde. And the *Journal Officiel* of the Commune is full of the nominations of bailiffs and, what is less gloomy, devotes three pages to the regulation of the ham fair.

As for the Bank of France, Jourde and Beslay's way of acting was unspeakable. Had it condemned Beslay, the Commune would have been afraid to see him leave, and he was considered indispensable at the Bank. And he was also a proof of honesty at the entrance to the Commune. Varlin, who rightly left a great reputation of uprightness and intelligence made too many allowances for Beslay. Jourde was not without value, but he unfortunately had some financial capacities. Have they bored us enough, these honest men and these financiers?

Q: *Did you believe in Paris's victory?*
A: At best, Paris could have won out over Versailles. But to believe that would have implied that the triumph of the social revolution would be naïve, for the Prussians weren't far away, and the provinces were around us. No, there was nothing to hope for. The frame of mind was not what it is today. If Paris were to proclaim the Commune today it would find partisans in every village of France.

Q: *During the final week?*
A: I was in the eleventh arrondissement at the barricade on the Rue Fontaine-au-Roi with Gambon, the two Ferrés, Géresme, Lacord[12] of the Central Committee, and Penet, a wood sculptor

---

11. Francis Jourde (1843–1893)—Accountant. Freemason. Member of the Commune for the fifth arrondissement. Member of the finance commission. Author of the decree on the postponing of payments due, the National Pawn Shop, and pensions for widows of fallen National Guardsmen. Attacked for being too respectful of the money held in the Bank of France. Sentenced to deportation in New Caledonia, escaped with Grousset and Rochefort.
12. Emile Lacord (1838–?)—Chef. One of the International's most active members. Failed in his election to the Commune. Continued his socialist

who is still alive today. There and elsewhere I could see that in the streets Paris had no better defenders than the very young and the elderly. Even more, since its inception, the insurrection had given rise to much heroism: it had Duval, Herpin-Lacroix, and Dombrowski, the Dombrowski to whom I one day said, "Look, you are needlessly exposing yourself; you're going to get yourself killed," and who, rolling a cigarette answered, "Not at all; but I have to show these good people that the General of the Commune is not afraid." And with him that wasn't a pose but rather the intrepidness of a hero of legend. And at the final barricades we saw Lisbonne offering himself as a target to the bullets, seated on a workhorse as big as an elephant and who, pointing to his men, replied to those who called to him, "I can't get down; this is the way they love me."

All this is perhaps secondary and the interest of so much Communard intrepidity seems to be of a decorative order. We lacked more precious qualities: initiative and the hatred of consecrated things.

GASTON DA COSTA

Former chief of cabinet of the Committee of Public Safety, former assistant prosecutor of the Commune, currently reader in a major bookstore, author of the grammar book adopted by the city of Paris for its schools

Q: *What was your role during the Commune?*
A: The Blanquist party, of which I was a member, was primarily represented during the Commune by men of action such as Eudes, Granger, Girault, Fortin, Rigault, Trinquet, Regnard, Ferré, Breuillé, Brideau, Jeunesse, Genton, etc. Many were members of the Committee of Public Safety.

The latter reorganized the prefecture of police in the same way that it had previously functioned and as it still functions

---

activities in exile. Died in Paris in extreme poverty, selling fried potatoes on the streets.

today, except that it was mainly occupied with political policing. I was particularly charged with the seeking out of former secret agents of the Imperial police. A certain number, who plotted alongside us under the Empire, were arrested, and the rest, declared hostages, were executed during the final days of the Bloody Week. I ran their pre-trial investigations and testified against them when they appeared before the revolutionary assizes whose juries were made up of delegates selected from the battalions of the Federals. This court had to judge, or rather declare to be or not to be hostages, policemen, priests, Municipal Guards, and individuals like Jecker, the man behind the war in Mexico. Once declared hostages, in keeping with the decree they had to be executed. In fact, the decree wasn't applied in the way it was written (three hostages were to be executed for each National Guardsman executed on the front lines).

Nevertheless, during the Bloody Week several hostages were executed at La Roquette and on the Rue Haxo. They were held either at Mazas or at La Roquette. On May 25 both the Place de la Bastille and Austerlitz Bridge were attacked by the Versaillais. Mazas was threatened. I received the order of the Commune, which at the time was taking refuge at the town hall of the eleventh arrondissement. The order, signed by Ferré, said to go to Mazas to carry out the transfer of the hostages from Mazas to La Roquette. This transfer was carried out in wagons that I requisitioned from the Compagnie de Lyon (it was the receipts that later caused my condemnation). While passing through the faubourg Saint-Antoine the wagons were attacked and, despite the escort, the crowd, made up mostly of women, wanted to lynch the hostages.

We had all the trouble in the world in getting to La Roquette. My role ended there. The next day Archbishop Darboy, Deguerry, several priests, and Jecker were executed. One shouldn't hasten to accuse the crowd of cowardice. One might say that this was a case of legitimate exasperation. You have to have lived the events to realize their state of mind. At the same spot the crowd, despite Delescluze and Eudes, had just executed the Count de Beaumont, who it accused of having misled it concerning the fate of a large number of dead in Neuilly.

I told you that I managed to save my convoy.

Q: *Even so, without hesitation you executed Ferré's order, even though you had foreseen the consequences.*
A: Exactly. What do you expect? We were living through a revolutionary torment. It was part of the struggle, the result of legitimate exasperation. These women were no more harpies than I was a bandit.

Q: *And the other hostages?*
A: Were transferred under the care of the chief judge of the court-martial to the Rue Haxo when Père Lachaise was threatened. On the Rue Haxo it was said that forty were executed. They were mostly secret agents, Municipal Guards, the Municipal Guards in civilian clothes. Most had been taken in the barracks and died bravely. There were almost no more priests on the Rue Haxo; the ones they were after were the police and the police informers. The people, the masses, didn't understand the meaning of the word hostage and naïvely translated it as priest, agent.

Q: *What else did you do?*
A: I signed all the arrest warrants. I am speaking, of course, only of arrests carried out regularly. But another fact contributed to my condemnation. It relates to Ruault, condemned under the empire in the Opera Comique Afffair, a plot against the Emperor in which, if I'm not mistaken, M. Ranc was accused. We all considered Ruault an old republican. When we had the proof that he was an agent you can imagine our indignation. When he was brought into my office I wrote some words on the back of his warrant that I showed him: "Save this canaille for the firing squad." The director of Mazas, a Blanquist as well, upon receiving this warrant placed it in his wallet. When I had the hostages evacuated from Mazas I had all the arrest warrants burned in the prison court-yard. Fifteen minutes after our departure the Versaillais entered, executed the director, found Ruault's warrant and my note.

Q: *How old were you?*
A: Twenty.

Q: *And the organization?*

A: I repeat: as far as I know only the personnel had changed at the prefecture of police.

In general, what the Blanquists wanted was a military dictatorship with the aim of defeating the Versaillais, to have a national convention named, and to continue the war. And this is why we expended all our efforts in trying to obtain Blanqui's exchange or escape.

All the offers of hostage exchange with Blanqui were sent from the prefecture of police, by the intermediary of Flotte, an old friend of Blanqui's. We offered all the hostages for Blanqui alone. We wanted to make Blanqui the leader of the insurrection. We didn't want to concern ourselves with parliamentary organization, administration, or socialism. Our sole objective was to go to Versailles, whose government was nothing but an usurper in our eyes. From this flowed the sortie of April 3: Eude's movements on Meudon in the center, of Flourens on the right wing on Bougival, and of Duval on the left on Chatillon. The goal of this movement was to take Versailles, to dissolve the Assembly and continue the war. Revolutionary republicans, we didn't conduct ourselves like a government in struggle with another government but like insurgents against usurpers who, above all, we had to overthrow.

Q: *Did these projects materialize differently from the sorties you spoke to us about?*

A: Between Rossel and the principal Blanquist leaders, it was question of carrying out a *coup d'état* with the aim of a military dictatorship, the sole manner in our opinion, of fighting and ceasing to deliberate. I recall a meeting held at the prefecture of police. We soon renounced our projects, seeing that it was too late. The proposal came from Rossel and was made just a few days before his resignation.

Q: *And your opinion on the Commune, on its influence?*

A: Well, when, after we returned after eight years of the penal colony, we saw the republic that had been made for us, we had to say that it wasn't worth the trouble.

MAXIME VUILLAUME

At the time editor of the Père Duchêne, *currently editor of the* Radical

Q: *As someone sentenced to death by the military provost of the Luxembourg, can you tell us how justice was rendered during the last week of May?*

A: My day was May 25. That day I heard many interrogations, which didn't take up too much of my time. Here was the formula: the provost asked, "You were arrested. Where?" "In my house tonight. I don't know why." The provost raised his eyes. And invariably, without any other explanation, "Put him in the line." Or more simply, with a glance at the door where four soldiers were standing, "In line!" Even so, for me it was a bit longer. I had been arrested on the street and I had the armband of the Cross of Geneva. "Why do you have that armband?" "I'm a doctor," I answered, "That's why I have the armband of the International Society for the Wounded, presided over by the Count of Flavigny. I was already a doctor during the siege." "And whose doctor are you now? Which wounded do you care for?" "All of them," I answered, embarrassed. "I cared for everyone during the battle, the soldiers of the army and those of the Commune" "You're not an army doctor?" "No, but . . ." "You remained in Paris during the Commune?" "Yes." The provost leaned over to the assistant and then, addressing the agents, said, "Take that man to the line."

Q: *And this "line," what was it?*

A: It was this. I left escorted by two agents with tricolor armbands. I found myself in the small courtyard of the senate. We turned to the left and an unforgettable spectacle suddenly appeared before me. Squeezed against a wall and surrounded by soldiers was a mass of men. Upon my arrival the ranks opened and then closed. This was what the provost called the line. Every few minutes a platoon of soldiers arrived and took away the first six. We then heard explosions. Hundreds and hundreds and hundreds of poor devils were executed in this way. There are piles of corpses under the two big gardens, and probably the body of Raoul Rigault.

Q: *And yet you're here.*

A: Thanks to the intercession of a sergeant of those troops who was a medical student: group solidarity!

Q: *But you weren't a doctor!*

A: Not in the least. I was editor of the *Père Duchêne* with Alphonse Humbert and Vermersch, and I had fought at the barricade on the Rue Monge. But if I really would have been a doctor, or even a supporter of Versailles, things would have gone the same way, except I would perhaps have been executed.

ELISÉE RECLUS[13]

My role during the Commune was officially nonexistent. I found myself among the anonymous mass of combatants and the defeated. A simple National Guardsman during the first days of the fight and then, after April 5 and for a year, a prisoner in the prisons of Satory, Trébéron, Brest, St-Germain, Versailles, and Paris, I can only formulate an opinion on the Commune from hearsay and the subsequent study of documents and men.

In the first years that followed the Commune it seemed to me that all those who had taken part in the movement were united due to the repression and the outrage suffered in common. I would not at that time have allowed myself to judge men who, in my opinion, were not worthy of the cause they defended. But the time has come to speak the truth, since impartial histories are beginning to be written and it is a matter of gathering information with future events in mind. I can thus affirm that during the first days of the Commune the military organization was as grotesque and worthless as it was during the first siege under

---

13. Elisée Reclus (1830–1905)—World-renowned geographer and early follower of Bakunin. Member of the National Guard, he was captured during the failed sortie of April 3. Sentenced to ten years banishment by a military tribunal. Returned to France in 1890 and was a tireless propagandist for anarchy till his death.

the leadership of the pitiful Trochu. The proclamations were as bombastic, the disorder as great, the actions as ridiculous.

We can confirm this from this simple fact: General Duval, who was on the plateau of Chatillon with two thousand men lacking in food and munitions, and who was surrounded by the growing mass of Versaillais, had requested reinforcements. We beat the call to arms in our arrondissement near the Pantheon, and at about 5:00 approximately six hundred men were gathered on the square. Full of ardor, we wanted to march immediately to the fight, along with other corps sent by the southern quarters of Paris. But it appears that this movement would not have been in conformity with military precedent, and we were led to the Place Vendôme where, deprived of any food or camping equipment, for more than half the night we had no other comfort than hearing the brilliant officers of the new general staff say from within the nearby ministry: "Drink, drink to the independence of the world!"

At 2:00 a.m. an order from the general made our troop, already largely diminished through desertion, leave the precarious shelter of the Place Vendôme, and we were taken to the Place de la Concorde, where we tried to sleep on the stones until 6:00 a.m. It was then that we were led to Chatillon, our bones broken by this first bivouac and without any food. During the march our little band continued to melt away, and though we were six hundred on our departure, fifty arrived on the plateau a half-hour before the Versaillais troops, pretending to go over to the cause of the revolution, were helped to climb the ramparts to repeated cries of "We are brothers! Let's embrace! Vive la République!" We were taken prisoner, and all those recognized by their uniform or their bearing as having once been soldiers were executed near the fence of the neighboring castle.

According to what my companions told me, I have every reason to believe that in other acts of war our gallant chiefs, at least those who commanded the first sorties, demonstrated the same lack of intelligence and the same negligence. Perhaps the government of the Commune had more capacities in other areas; in any case, history will say that these improvised ministers remained honest in exercising their power. But we asked something else of them: to have the good sense and determination that the situation required and to act in consequence. It was with real shock that we watched them continue all the same errors of official governments: maintaining the whole state governing system while only changing the men, keeping in place the entire bureaucracy, allowing tax agents to function in their booths and protect the money that the Bank of France sent to Versailles? The vertigo of power and the spirit of stupid routine had seized hold of them, and these men, who should have acted heroically and known how to die, had the inconceivably shameful naïveté to address diplomatic notes to the great powers in a style of which Metternich and Talleyrand would have approved. They understood nothing of the revolutionary movement that had carried them through the doors of the Hôtel de Ville.

But what the chiefs didn't know to do, the nameless crowd did. There were many of them, thirty to forty thousand perhaps, who died around Paris for the cause they loved. There were many as well who, within the city, fell before the machine guns, shouting "Vive la Commune!" We know from the first days of the Assembly in Versailles that this slaughtered people by its attitude saved the republican form of French government. Nevertheless, the present republic, a servant in the service of the Tsar and the Kaiser, is so far from any practice of liberty that it would be childish to be grateful to the Commune for its having saved this vain word for us. But it did something else. It held before us for the future, not through its rulers but through its defenders, an ideal far superior to that of all the revolutions that had preceded it. It commits in advance those who want to continue it—in France and throughout the world—to fight for a new society in which there will be neither masters by birth, titles, or money, nor servants by origin, caste, or salary. Everywhere the word "Commune" was understood in the widest sense, as having to do with a new humanity, formed of free and equal companions, ignorant of the existence of ancient borders, and assisting each other in peace from one end of the world to the other.

A REBEL FROM LYON

My role, from September 4 to March 22, was that of an ardent propagandist of the revolution, preaching in the workshop, involving myself with every movement, all the little riots that took place between these two dates. This attitude got me elected member of the Lyon Commune. Instinctively, through intuition rather than through reasoning, I felt that I was guilty of illogic by preaching freedom and accepting to be a new master. But how could I refuse without being taken for a coward? There was danger and I accepted it. I have been angry at myself ever since, though at that time I was one of those who believed that something could be done by a revolutionary government. I hadn't yet understood that if the revolution isn't created first as an idea, it's not possible as an action, and consequently, if it is made and passes into ideas it is pointless to elect a government to make it succeed. This was so logical that I hadn't even thought of it.

My role on the Commune was the same as any ruler's: it was absolutely useless when it wasn't harmful. I was delegate for public works, which almost earned me delegation to forced labor. I thought it would be easy to sweep away Versaillais reaction, represented by Andrieux, Barodet, Gailleton, Perret, and Le Royer, among others, all of whom were later rewarded for their attitude during that period. I thought it would be enough to call on the people who had just mandated us to carry out this cleanup and they would come to the rescue. But they thought that their effort in electing the revolutionary Commune was enough, and they relied on us, who could do nothing without them. Three days passed with each of us counting on the other, at the end of which we all fell asleep, only to wake up with the red flag lowered and the tricolor flying.

Why this impotence on one hand and abandonment on the other? There were two causes for this. Paris, when it started to act on March 18, at first only called for its autonomy. But Lyon already had this communal autonomy, and because of this had difficulties in supporting Paris. Reaction didn't fail to exploit this situation, saying that Lyon had no reason to rebel in order to obtain what it already had. The agitation was carried out in a void, since the argument convinced a good number of people and Paris sent us its delegates *before* the timid reforms that it later demanded were implemented. Despite the people's ignorance and their faith in their rulers, the results would have been completely different if they had waited for the reforms proposed by the Paris Commune. Perhaps Lyon would have abandoned the communalist idea and taken up the economic idea, and then, having a clear field of action, things would have been different. But there you have it; at the time we waited for the Paris initiative, and it came too late.

The other cause of impotence resided in the absence of material and moral force on our part. Despite the proclamation of the Commune, reaction was still the master of Lyon because it held all the forts, which as everyone knows were built with nothing but an internal revolution in mind. It had the army and it had the money, which is what allowed it to function, for in fleeing and saving itself it had saved the cash box. On our side, we had the rifles of the National Guard and some cartridges, plus a pitiful little fort with its spiked cannons. Facing the army in these conditions could only have produced a useless hecatomb.

A member of the Commune told us that we had the canals and the torch at our disposal and that, not being able to seize the owners—who had sought refuge with the army—we could take what was their strength and our weakness: property. We could do this by calling on the people to act like communist revolutionaries, to leave their shacks to live in the empty luxurious palaces and houses, to eat their fill by expropriating the accumulated foodstuffs, to dress themselves by using the products woven by them and held by the Jews—in Christian or other form—and in this way they would attain two goals. The first was that of meting out justice, and the second that of leading Versailles to dismember the army that was before Paris and thus unblock that city. But either the word "communism" may have spread fear, or it was judged that popular morality was not yet ripe for these demands. The motion was rejected, and as a result we didn't roast property; it was property that let us stew in our own juices.

I was foolish enough to accept a power that tied my hands while giving me the right to tie those of others. I here make my mea culpa; I would never make that mistake today.

My opinion is that the insurrection of 1871 could not succeed, precisely because it left the insurrectionary state behind in order to enter the governmental state. I believe that any insurrection that marches to the conquest of a new government is sterile; that any insurrection that names chiefs is stillborn. The insurrectionary state is one in which the people alone, without leaders or chiefs, can specify its desires, its wishes, its aspirations and its needs. As soon as there is a chief, there is a master; the insurrectionary state comes to an end and gives way to slavery. And it is idiocy to say that you can give yourselves chiefs who will command you to go to Versailles because you command them to lead you. Paris, Lyon, and the other Communes of 1871 died because of their chiefs, of parliamentarians, even the best intentioned. Whether we want it or not, things are and always will be thus.

The influence of these insurrections is great precisely because of their defeat. Until then the provinces were used to following Paris, and they believed themselves powerless if Paris didn't take the initiative. They didn't believe themselves to be a force without Paris; there was a kind of centralization of brains toward which everything radiated. Paris seemed to be the center of this radiance. In a way we acted as we would under a form of militarism, where everything is concentrated on one point, everything seems good if this center is the victor, but everything seems and is defective if it is vanquished. It is then that the guerrilla army begins to form, which, with its small numbers, succeeds where a larger army couldn't. A defeated Paris, having in hand an imposing force and seeking to create communal guerrillas, proved to the provinces that even alone they are a force. They no longer wait for Paris to give them ideas; they break themselves up into smaller groups in order to advance more quickly. As proof of this I only have to give the trials and sentencing that took place in the provinces well before those of Paris, the trial in Lyon having preceded that of the Thirty in Paris.

Political and administrative decentralization has been spoken of; the decentralization of brains followed. If we were to investigate, if we were to ask provincial revolutionaries what they would do today if similar events were to occur, there would be a unanimous response: we wouldn't accept battle with soldiers who, after all, are our kind. We would fight against wealth, and if we couldn't pinch the owner we would wipe out what constitutes his joy and his strength. We would flee, leaving nothing standing behind us. People add, with some reason, that they believe that they wouldn't be forced to go to these extremes, and that as soon as the forward march would begin the frightened bourgeoisie would come to its senses. Are they right in all this?

Whatever the case, these ideas are born under the influence of the defeats of the working class. I believe that several insurrections at once at several points are possible, all marching toward the same goal, toward the satisfaction of material needs *before* that of moral needs, something I wouldn't have thought possible before '71. Unlike that period, today the people know full well that it is a matter of indifference to them whether they are taught to read that there is much wheat in America if they are prevented from eating it. They know that if their bellies are empty that it makes no difference to them to know that the moon transmits thirteen times less light than we transmit to it. They want to live, and to live well, since they produce everything. They thought they could obtain this well-being through political revolutions; our defeats have shown them that they can't. If the defeats have done nothing but demonstrate this they would be worth it.

To finish, I confess to having many regrets that I couldn't do more. But my most crushing regret is that of having deserved this terrible slap in the face: I was in exile, arguing with Jacques Gross, who has since become one of my best friends, when he threw this in my face: Shut up, elected representative!

P-O LISSAGARAY[14]

M. Lissagaray wrote The History of the Commune of 1871 *in six hundred thoroughly documented pages. There was thus no call for a long interview. We first asked him for some anecdotes.*

Q: *Did women have a role?*
A: We see many of them behind the barricades. As for the *pétroleuses* (women accused of setting fire to Paris during the Commune's final days), these were chimerical beings, like salamanders and elves. The military tribunals didn't succeed in exhibiting a single one. These tribunals sentenced many women, few of whom had been widely known during the events. Louise Michel was an exception. In front of the judges she was as aggressive as she was in battle and took on the role of accuser. Another, whose name was Dimitriev, was a fantastic creature on a tragic background. She came from Russia, where she had left her husband. During the Commune she was seen in a fabulous red dress, her belt crenellated with pistols. She was twenty years old and beautiful. She had adorers but either "the bare-armed" didn't please her behind closed doors or, for her, love was an exclusively feminine sport, and no one could melt this young ice cube. And it was chastely that she took the wounded Frankel in her arms on the barricades, for she was at the barricades, where her bravery was charming. We must mention her attire: a fancy outfit of black velvet.

Q: *She was seized?*
A: No, and a few weeks later she was installed in Switzerland. Quite wealthy, she had a hotel on the banks of the lake and nursed refugees. In her salons there was a brilliant society of "forced laborers" and other exoticisms, along with a few men under the death penalty. She then returned to Russia to rejoin her husband, who died soon thereafter. There was a trial where she appeared as a witness. The lord had apparently been poisoned. The overseer

---

14. Prosper-Olivier Lissagaray (1838–1901)—Journalist and writer. Fought at the barricades and edited two newspapers under the Commune. In exile grew close to Eleanor Marx, who translated his *History of the Paris Commune of 1871*. Later active in the fight against Boulanger and in support of Dreyfus.

was sent to Siberia, where she hastened to join him. No one ever heard from her again.

Q: *How would you summarize the causes of the fall of the Commune?*

A: The capital errors of the beginning were not having occupied Mont-Valérien and having waited until April 3 to march on Versailles. The Central Committee's interference in affairs after the elections, the manifesto/split of the twenty-two of the minority (May 15), and the Commune's mania to legislate when it should have been fighting and preparing the final struggle were all seeds of the defeat. And once Versailles was inside Paris the defeat was hastened by Delescluze's proclamation of May 22 putting an end to any discipline through the dispersion of the members of the Commune in their neighborhoods (the defense was from that point on decapitated), by the virtual inaction of the artillery park of Montmartre, and by the burning down of the Hôtel de Ville. Before May 21, the day of the invasion, nothing, or almost nothing, had been done for the defense of the streets. They had offered 3 francs 75 to laborers but hadn't found any takers. They had laborers for free; they had an entire people during the tragic hours, but it was too late. Two hundred planned, strategic, and unified barricades were needed, which ten thousand men could have defended. We had hundreds and hundreds of barricades, but they were uncoordinated and impossible to man. Alas, the Commune hadn't spent money for its defense. Its munificence had only gone as gone as far as the daily 30 sous of the National Guardsmen. They should have put pressure on M. Thiers by seizing the Bank of France as a guarantee. There was no argument that would have been more decisive. Even more, in the Bank, among other docile riches, there were blue bills with a value of nine hundred million that only waited for an engraver to be put in circulation. It is truly sad that in the course of an insurrection that counted so many workers in the arts that one wasn't found.

ALPHONSE HUMBERT[15]

At the time editor of Père Duchêne, *since then president of the Paris Municipal Council and currently deputy*

I consider the Commune a heroic act; this and nothing else, for I don't think it marked a date in the history of socialism.

Q: *Can you give us some anecdotic details on the final days?*
A: The Thursday of the final week, May 25, I was with Lissagaray, Jourde, Larochelle, the Commune member Johannard, etc., on the barricade at the entry to the Boulevard Voltaire. Delescluze had just died; over the barricade we could see his corpse. I remember that we had among us a big, colorful lad, a kind of rustic gentleman who in the midst of the flying projectiles shouted, "And to think I came to Paris to have some fun." He was shot in the calf. It was 5:00 or 6:00 P.M.; the barricade, being untenable, was evacuated. The firing from the barracks occupied by the soldiers swept the boulevard. We answered them from a balcony. There was a variety of faces there, among which I recall Johannard in a state of mad exasperation.

Q: *And the following day?*
A: The evening of the following day, while returning from I don't remember where and going up to Belleville, Jourde, Lissagaray, the medical student Dubois, and I met a group of National Guardsmen. One of them, Carria the younger, told us, "We're going to relieve the gendarmes." I think he was alluding to the Parisian gendarmes from the Roquette quarter. A little later, in the Lake Saint Fargeau quarter, we were dining at the Lapin Vengeur when we heard rifle shots. Suddenly it hit me: "My God, those are the gendarmes that are being executed." The hotel owner came in with a plate of rabbit in his hands, into which tears were falling. I wasn't wrong; it was the hostages. We were only a few steps away from the Rue Haxo.

Q: *Once the Hôtel de Ville was evacuated, did the members of the Commune personally take part in the defense of the barricades?*

---

15. Alphonse Humbert (1844–1922)—Militant Blanquist. Journalist at *Le Père Duchêne*. After his return from exile was a Radical Socialist deputy and municipal councilor.

A: Almost all of them, which is something unique in the history of governments. They set an example of intrepidity. What a generation!

Q: *How were these fighters of the final moments able to avoid falling into the hands of the Versaillais?*
A: It was relatively easy to leave during the battle, but afterward the exits from every neighborhood were guarded by soldiers, and when you arrived at them you had to submit to an interrogation. After adventures and alerts, Lissagaray and I were able to leave via the eleventh arrondissement, thanks to a curvaceous and jovial hotel keeper. That night we asked Suzanne Lagier to put us up and she refused. We had to look elsewhere. For several days we went from place to place, and then Lissagaray was able to leave Paris. As for me, I was captured two weeks later after having been denounced by a concierge. I have since learned that she was condemned by a military tribunal for having turned in Versaillais soldiers during the Commune.

Q: *Do you think that one of the results of the Commune was the maintaining of the republic?*
A: Yes, since after the execution of the Commune, the period during which it would have been propitious to execute the republic had passed.

Q: *Were those of you at the Père Duchêne favorable to the majority or the minority on the Commune?*
A: Vermersch to the majority, Vuillaume and I more or less to the minority. The latter was made up of the most intelligent men, but I now recognize that the revolutionaries of the majority, with their less theoretical bent and their decisiveness, saw things more clearly.

Q: *What is your opinion of the military leaders?*
A: Cluseret was a poseur. His thing was to show that he was brave (and he was) and to impress the National Guardsmen. When Federals brought him bad news or asked for reinforcements he calmly answered them, "Go back, boys, I've got things under control. Everything is fine." The men went back saying, "What a man; what calm." He would then pick up his pipe and,

comfortably seated in his easy chair, would stretch his legs under the table. As for Rossel, he was a religious fanatic and a patriot. Without being a professional soldier in the worst sense of the term, he didn't much believe in the National Guard, and in fact during the two months of struggle almost the entire military effort was borne by eight to ten thousand men of the free corps.

The Commune couldn't introduce discipline among its troops; it couldn't quarrel with anyone. Rigorous acts of repression were impossible for it. For me, Bergeret was a faker. Eudes was completely unaware of his role. His bravery, like that of Duval, was amazing. Dombrowski was used to war on the barricades. He was an admirable leader and was brave as a Pole. Was he listening to Versailles's proposals? Did he want to fool the enemy? Wanting to clear himself of any suspicion, he got himself killed at the barricade on the Rue Myrrha. Wroblewski was very intelligent, La Cécilia very brave, but he lost his head when faced with the responsibilities of command.

Q: *And from a financial point of view?*
A: Jourde wasn't a high financier, but a precise and honest accountant. He limited his role to distributing to the arrondissements the money that was indispensable. Beslay wasn't able to take full advantage of the bank.

Q: *And life in New Caledonia?*
A: Sinister beyond words. Nevertheless, there was a glimmer of hope when Grévy was elected to the presidency. We were invited to submit requests for pardon, and we were promised they would be accepted. Those sentenced to simple deportation were, but this was less the case for those sentenced to deportation to a fortified place. Where I was, in the penal colony, there were almost none; these were the most compromised men. In the colony there were workers, the humble who didn't have to pretend because they were hoping for a seat at municipal councilor or deputy, and they wrote furiously indignant letters in response to the offer.

I have maintained a profound admiration for the anonymous mass that defended the Commune. The leaders were no less courageous. I can still see Jaclard on horseback and in the uniform of a colonel in the Commune's final moments when disguise was needed in order to flee. Yes, they were all intrepid, cheerfully so and without posturing.

G. LEFRANÇAIS[16]
Member of the Commune

The degrading situation that the French Republic now finds itself in—a situation wanted by all those who have held the government in their hands since September 4, 1870, faithful continuators of the system inaugurated by the republicans of February 24, 1848—clearly proves that the proletariat has nothing to hope for from those who don't recognize that revolution and authority, be it republican or royalist, are antagonistic.

This was this profound conviction held by most of those who composed the minority of the Commune of 1871 that led them to separate from their Jacobin colleagues, while recognizing their sincerity and their devotion to the revolution of March 18.

The twenty-five years that have passed have convinced me even more that the minority was right and that the proletariat will only succeed in truly emancipating itself on the condition that it rid itself of the republic, the last, and not the least maleficent form of authoritarian governments.

But if it persists in its mad hope of arriving at its emancipation through the famous "conquest of governmental power" it is certainly preparing for itself a new and bloody disappointment from which it will likely not recover for quite some time.

---

16. Gustave Lefrançais (1826–1901)—Schoolteacher and accountant. Member of the International. Member of the Commune, representing the fourth arrondissement. Member of the Commune's executive and labor commissions. Fought on the barricades at the Bastille and the Arsenal during Bloody Week. In exile in Switzerland sided with the Bakuninists in their fight with the Marxists in the International. Eugene Pottier dedicated "The Internationale" to Lefrançais.

M. BRUNEL [17]

Currently professor at the Dartmouth Naval School

1. Named chief of the 107th Battalion on March 19, 1870, successive acts of war led me to be General-in-Chief of the Central Committee head of the 10th Legion and then member of the Commune. The principal events I participated in were the taking of the barracks of the Chateau-d'Eau and the occupation of the Hôtel de Ville on the afternoon and evening of March 18 and the seizing of the ministries on March 19.

(During the German war I took part in the defense of the fort of Issy and the capture and occupation of the heights of Buzenval, despite the attacks by the Prussian troops. For this feat of war I was proposed for the cross, but I refused.)

When we had to retreat, surrounded on all sides by houses in flames and troops that threatened our retreat, we occupied the tenth arrondissement and then the barracks of the Place de la République where a wound led to my removal from the battlefield.

If I add that I was sentenced to the death penalty then I will have finished with all that concerns me.

2. The insurrection of 1871 is still misunderstood. It was first provoked by a patriotic sentiment and by the determination to prevent the monarchical form of government from taking possession of the country. Almost all the men placed at the head of the movement proved themselves before the enemy and actively professed republican ideas.

The starting point was thus patriotism and the republic.

Could we have succeeded, and why were we defeated?

In a revolution it doesn't suffice to have generous tendencies and to count too much on the enthusiasm of the masses. If we fight against hardened troops we must know how to imitate what constitutes their strength, and even surpass them in valor and discipline. A scattered command cannot hope for victory, and this is what the Commune didn't understand.

17. Antoine Brunel (1830–?)—Career officer. Member of the Commune representing the seventh arrondissement. General of the National Guard. Participated in the final defense of Paris.

Made up of men whose sincerity was indisputable, but whose heads were filled with ideas and who understood nothing about how to conduct a war, the Commune unfortunately suffered the influence that can be seen in all political bodies. Instead of constituting a mighty political power it failed to ensure unity of action and gradually allowed all its forces—the 250,000 men who made up the defense of Paris—to be dispersed.

3. The Commune preserved a republican center in monarchical Europe.

It gave the people of Europe a banner.

It raised an insurmountable barrier between the two social forms.

Its hecatombs showed the entire world what the enemies of progress and all great reforms were capable of doing.

It also showed that blood and steel alone can smash age-old obstacles and give birth to a new society.

This anticipated revolution, which is only a precursor, clearly shows apparently degenerate France that it can no longer hope for anything from the men who govern it.

We have gone from defeat to defeat since 1870. Formerly powerful, we are now nothing but satellites.

And is if nature has abandoned us, we increasingly lack the force to reproduce.

But all of this is due to the causes inherent in the regime we allowed ourselves to be governed by. Once these causes are destroyed we will resume our place in Europe. Imminent events will complete this metamorphosis; we will no longer commit the same errors as in the past, for we now know where we want to go.

LÉO MEILLET[18]

Member of the Commune, currently a professor in Edinburgh

Your questions require a lengthy analysis which I am not able to provide, first because I don't have the time, and then because, leading a retired life and having spent twenty-five years outside of France, I've never thought of coordinating my memories or analyzing my impressions.

From March 18 until the end of May, I was overloaded with work. As deputy mayor of the thirteenth arrondissement and charged with administering my district on my own I participated in many meetings with my colleagues at the town hall of the second arrondissement on the Rue de la Banque. And then on the Commune, little by little I accumulated the functions of a member of the justice commission, of the external relations commission, president of the appeals court of the courts-martial, quaestor of the Commune, member of the first Committee of Public Safety, governor of the fort of Bicêtre, civil commissioner delegated to the southern army, all the while administering my arrondissement, a task in which my colleagues took no part.

You can easily understand that everything is jumbled up in my head. Nevertheless, in order to cooperate as much as possible in the speedy publication of your investigation, I will risk sending you the few reflections that particularly come to mind.

I consider the revolution of March 18 an entirely spontaneous manifestation of popular instinct. It was the unthinking surge of a people that felt itself betrayed and threatened, but whose forward march, instead of being based on an analysis of its sufferings and the consciousness of its needs, had no other guide than the abstractions of historical memory and vague ideal aspirations. This is enough in order to fight and die heroically, but not enough to triumph and live. All of our errors are summed up

---

18. Léo Meillet (1843–1909)—Law clerk. Freemason. Member of the International. Member of the Commune, elected by the thirteenth arrondissement. Member of the justice and external relations commissions and the first Committee of Public Safety. Sentenced to death in absentia. Elected deputy in 1898 as an independent socialist.

in these words: "Not to know," with their mandatory corollary, "Not to dare."

It's because the Central Committee *didn't know* that from the time it entered the Hôtel de Ville its only concern was to leave it and it *didn't dare* to attempt (and this was something quite possible at that moment) to revolutionarily take control of Paris and take hold of Versailles before Thiers could assemble his army. A revolution that begins by legislating for ten days is condemned to death, and the Commune could have no other end than that of being the registry room of the people's defeat.

The hesitations and tergiversations of the Commune can also be attributed to this same initial defect. Born of the interminable negotiations of the second half of March, at the beginning it lacked the revolutionary sentiment that progressively developed within it as its fall became imminent and which, had it been produced earlier, could have delayed its defeat by several weeks.

In the absence of documents, and only having vague memories at my disposal, I don't dare risk speaking of the Commune's parliamentary, military, financial, or administrative organization, but it is my opinion that if, from the revolutionary point of view, it left much to be desired, it can be compared positively—except from the military point of view—to all the governments that preceded and followed it. And the honesty and disinterestedness of the members of the Commune and most of its agents is only contested by parvenus of letters and pillars of the bank and the sacristy.

I can't speak about the influence of the Commune on events and ideas; I'm afraid I'd be led astray by my personal sympathies. And yet, it can't be hidden that it was very great. It is generally admitted that in France it saved, if not the republic, at least the republican form. The duration of the resistance and the immense massacre that marked its epic end have drawn the attention of even the slowest to be moved of proletarians, and the thousands of exiles that its fall scattered around the civilized globe have constituted so many rings destined to connect France to the great international socialist movement.

NADAR

To the right of the boulevards there came a sound that was distant, intense, deep. As it grew nearer, the sound grew louder by the minute, and the crescendo exploded beneath us. Something extraordinary was surely happening.

The people in the apartment all rushed to the windows. Sick and, unbeknownst to me, condemned by the doctors, I dragged myself to the window as well, driven by an unhealthy contagion of curiosity for which I would be punished.

After so much pain, sorrow, and horror, here is what I saw and heard in the middle of Paris, the center of human civilization.

Behind a platoon of chasseurs on horseback, their muskets upright on their thighs, between two rows of horsemen there filed endlessly, four by four in the middle of the street, an uncountable number of men. Prisoners grabbed individually or in sweeps, sometimes based on their appearance, or on the look of their shoes, or on nothing, on the whims of choice. There were neither women nor children in this convoy. But there were many young soldiers, their caps inside out, from the two regiments which, engaged deep within Paris, were forgotten there on March 18 by their chiefs as they fled to Versailles. These men couldn't leave once Paris was evacuated by the civil and military governments, since the strictest rules forbade the departure through the gates of Paris of any man under forty.

Among these soldiers, now without chiefs and absolutely left to their own devices in the middle of a general insurrection, some had been incorporated into National Guard battalions. As was well known, others in large numbers resolutely refused to march against the Versailles troops and, as we learned from the newspapers, a special barracks had been granted them, after a stormy discussion in the Commune.

What exactly were those who, momentarily degraded, filed along before our eyes, while waiting for the rest of the men?

Which among them were faithful and which were enemies? What was the difference? They marched quickly, pushed along. Most had their heads bowed and alongside them was a confused mass of other prisoners of all kinds and dress: National Guardsmen, workers, bourgeois, marching under the deafening clamor of insults, jeers, and threats. The two rows of horsemen occasionally swayed under the terrible pressure of the spectators, protecting the captives with difficulty; men not sentenced, not judged, not even interrogated yet. Well-dressed men and ladies banged into each other, pushed each other so they could insult the prisoners from up close, these prisoners who were neither condemned, judged, nor tried. And at the height of the bloodthirsty madness, unanimously, without a protest, without challenge, they cried out, they shouted these terrible cries that I can still hear: "Death! Death! Don't take them any further! Here! Right now!"

How many pent up cowardly terrors had there been for them to be unleashed with such ferocity?

The prisoners continued to advance, seeming not to want either to see or hear. But one of them turned and cried out, waving his fist, "Cowards!" At that moment, like a rocket, an old and fat decorated gentleman, dressed respectably, flew from the Café de la Paix, and breaking through the crowd, beat the prisoners with his cane.

But all of this—shouts, threats, insults, screams—was still nothing. A formidable, deafening clamor burst out, and in this mass there was a furious movement where prisoners and escort seemed to mutually annihilate each other.

Above them all, there advanced like a ghost, pale, bloody, haggard, his hair standing on end, rocking side to side and supported on each side, a man wounded in the back, it was said and who, unable to march any longer, had been hoisted onto the horse of one of the men of the escort.

Who was this unfortunate? Was he really one of the leaders, or was he taken for one because he alone was on horseback? Whatever the case, the look of this moribund (he was going no further, we were told, than the church of the Madeleine) was able to accomplish the unlikely feat of further increasing the homicidal delirium of these lycanthropes.

And above the shouts and roars of the possessed, "Death! Here! Now!" we heard a strident voice from among them, the voice of a woman, shrieking toward the clouds in a falsetto, "Tear out their nails!"

Yes, this is what I saw, this is what I heard, in the middle of Paris, the center of world civilization.

And as a sincere, disinterested witness, with other similar testimony at hand, historically, as is my duty, I testify.

M. VICTOR JACLARD

Chief of the Seventeenth Legion

We asked M. Jaclard about the Central Committee. He answered:
The Central Committee made the mistake common to most governments that are the result of a revolution: it didn't dare. A popular movement is lost if it stops halfway. It was necessary to march on Versailles without stopping. I called for this from the first day. On March 26, having read in the *Journal Officiel* a note where there was talk of negotiating with Versailles I published a letter that ended with these words: "There is only one way to negotiate with Versailles, and that's to capture it." The sortie of April 2 decided upon by the Commune came too late. It would perhaps have succeed despite it all if the Central Committee, instead of listening to the declarations of a man who was mad before he was a sell-out had taken the trouble to ensure that Mont-Valérien was in the hands of the National Guard.

Remaining inactive while it was part of the government, the Central Committee felt the need to act when it no longer was there. After the elections to the Commune, attempting to seize a power it had just abdicated, it succeeded in creating duality in leadership and hindering the activity of the Commune.

On the military leaders:
Most of the generals of the Commune had served as officers in the foreign armies and without any doubt possessed a certain competence in military matters. But their common error was in not taking sufficient account of the quite strange nature of the

elements they had to lead. Rossel, who had proved himself during the Franco-Prussian War and who had a reputation for intelligence among the military leaders of the Commune, committed this singular error, just like anyone else, more than anyone else: he didn't understand that the incohesive mass of our battalions couldn't be handled like Prussian-style disciplined regiments, particularly at a moment when confidence in the leaders had been sorely tested. Rossel knew how to command but not how to be obeyed. Events proved this only too clearly. Instead of throwing contempt in the face of the National Guard he should have said a profound mea culpa for himself.

On the influence that Blanqui, had he been in Paris, could have had on events:
Would Blanqui have had enough authority to lead a march on Versailles on March 19? It's possible. Would he have had the needed decisiveness? I think so. In that case everything would have been different. Had things been the opposite he would have been, like so many others, an impotent force paralyzed by circumstances. Locked within Paris, the Commune was buried before it was dead.

But wasn't Blanqui hesitant in general?
Every revolutionary leader hesitates when it's a matter of throwing an organization onto the streets. He hesitates because the material means he disposes of are always disproportionate to the obstacle to be defeated. It is the unforeseen elements of circumstances and the impatience of the troops that more often than not decide for him.

How do you judge the attitude of the minority of the Commune?
My opinion is that a division among chiefs is always to be avoided on the battlefield, if for no other reason than its moral effect. It is even worse in that it can appear to be due to the fear of certain responsibilities. It gives most of the troops the impression of every man for himself. Leaders willingly forget that in time of revolution their personalities no longer count.

And the fires set by the Commune?
Arson is accepted as a means of defense according to the barbaric customs of war. The Commune's arson was wrong in that it was

so hasty that it served to shorten resistance instead of contributing to prolonging it.

You were at the barricades of the final days. Can you relate some episode that is characteristic of the barricades, the streets, and the houses?

M. Jaclard, not wanting to boast, hesitates. Upon our insisting, he tells us the following story. It has to do with Vermorel as much as with himself.

It was Thursday at 1:00 or 2:00. Vermorel, at the town hall of the eleventh arrondissement, said to me, "They tell me that the barricade of the Chateau-d'Eau is abandoned. Do you want to go there with me?" Along the way we brought together the debris of two battalions of my legion who had taken part throughout the life of the Commune in the hostilities around Asnières-Neuilly. We also met Lisbonne at the head of his general staff, and he and Vermorel had this dialogue: "What's happening over there?" "There's no longer any way to hold out." "We're going back; come with us." The whole general staff shouted, "No, that's impossible!" Lisbonne turned around his horse, which his officers were holding by the bridle. Vermorel then said, "I'm a member of the Commune and I order you to march!" And so we left with a handful of officers. Theisz, in the uniform of a National Guardsman, was with us. We distributed the men at the barricade. We passed the nearby barricades in review and managed to plug in the gaps. We found Ranvier at the one on the Rue Popincourt. All was quiet. Vermorel and I returned to the town hall of the eleventh arrondissement where we got the news form Varlin, who had assumed leadership of the defense at the Bastille. Vermorel said to me, "I'm exhausted. Before we go any further I'm going to take a bath. That'll refresh me." We had hardly taken a few steps outside the house when we again met up with men fleeing the barricade at the Chateau-d'Eau. We tried to rally them and then went back to the barricade. Vermorel said, "I've learned that they're going to blow up the houses on the corners. It doesn't bother you to be blown up with them?" He took a few steps away, and I saw him in the middle of the barricade. Theisz and Lisbonne were still there. Suddenly I heard, "Help me, Jaclard!" At the same moment, on the top of a barricade, a kid, flag in hand, was shouting at the Versaillais. A

National Guardsman was pulling him back. I held up Vermorel. I saw Lisbonne fall. I dragged Vermorel a few steps from there and, turning around, I saw the kid from the barricade. He was brought down. We reached the next street. I laid Vermorel out on the street. A camp follower, a beautiful young girl of seventeen, gave him something to drink and embraced him. When I raised my eyes I saw Delescluze standing gloomily before me. One of those accompanying him said, "Don't go any further." Delescluze didn't answer. They carried Vermorel on rifles to the town hall of the eleventh arrondissement. No one was left behind the barricade. All had fallen or vanished. A moment later I rejoined Vermorel and put a bandage on him. His thigh had been shot clear through near the hip.

During the evening I returned to the town hall and trans-ported to a house at the corner of the Boulevard Voltaire and the Place du Trône, where Olivier Pain's father lived. Ranvier, wearing his sash, was with us. We said to the concierge, "We're bring-ing in a friend of M. Pain." She went to tell him and came back, saying, "M. Pain wasn't even able to receive his wounded son." "Well then, if he can't receive our friend willingly he'll do so by force." To which she responded, "Don't get angry. We'll work it out somehow." And she took us to the second floor to a large, empty apartment.

Vermorel was laid on a mattress. That same evening we decided on the abandonment of the town hall in the morning and the retreat to Belleville. I went to Vermorel to tell him that I had to leave him. But the concierge wanted us to take him to the apartment across the hall on the same floor. There I put on his final bandage. The concierge burst in, shouting, "The Versaillais are in the house!" I was still wearing my uniform. She tore my clothing off me, tossed me her husband's, climbed to the attic to hide my clothes and came back down, called after by the Versaillais. The search began. There they were on the second floor. The door across the way opened. We heard a shot. They had killed a wounded *fédéré* who had been transported there once Vermorel had left. Without stopping at the other door they went upstairs. From the attic a soldier shouted, "A general's saber! The brigand fled, but we're sure to find him!" They went back downstairs. I had told my friend, "Play dead or at least the dying man." The doorbell rings. I open and find myself in front of the captain, some soldiers, and the concierge. "I'm madame's brother-in-law." She understands and throws herself at the captain's feet. "Yes, that's my brother-in-law. I beg you, don't hurt him." "Fine. Do you have any weapons?" "No." They enter. I take them everywhere except Vermorel's room. The captain says to me, "What are you doing in a house like this?' "I was away from Paris during the war and the Commune. I was worried about my sister-in-law and I came to see how she is." "But it's not possible to enter Paris." "It must be possible, since I'm here." "Fine. Stay here." And under his breath, "It's all the same. His face isn't categorical." He left, but to go into Vermorel's room. I heard the latter groan, "Can't you let me die in peace?" And a sergeant said, "Don't worry, we won't do you any harm." Fortunately they hadn't, as was usually the case, stripped the bed to see if the invalid wasn't wounded. I could no longer leave. The alerts must have continued. The concierge soon appeared. "Oh no, all is lost. The police superintendent is going to do a search." "Quick then, go find the captain." The concierge was a friendly and forward individual and I imagined that, even it was just her nature, she must have been on good terms with the military. "Tell him, my captain, what's going on? They're going to send the police to us? It's an indignity to send the police when you're here. You can't allow that!?" The stratagem worked.

Sunday morning, as we were impatient to know what was happening outside, I went to find Cère who had been Vermorel's secretary and who since then got a job at the Senate, which he perhaps still has. Cère said to me, "Did you read this morning's *Gaulois*? I read a note in it that said that Vermorel, who was said to have been killed, is only wounded and is now on the Boulevard Voltaire at such and such a number, with Jaclard, who's taking care of him." I immediately returned to our place sure that I wouldn't find Vermorel there. But he was there. I put a stiff bandage on him. He went down the stairs as best he could. There was a carriage in the courtyard. We left for the Monceau quarter where a capitalist lived who Vermorel had protected during the Commune and who had told him to make use of his home if he ever needed to. A domestic opened the door for us. "Monsieur left this morning with a pass from M. Thiers. "After negotiations we were set up in the cellar. At four in the morning the door opened. We found ourselves face to face with the troops. The sheets were torn from us. We were both taken to the provost's office on the Champs Elysées. Vermorel still had his bandage from the day before.

On the way we were able to cook up a story. Vermorel, being wounded, couldn't deny having fought. Such a good catch, a member of the Commune, could only be helped by making his name known. He was someone they'd want to save for the court-martial. As for me, I said I was a pharmacist friend of his called on to take care of him, and so was alongside him. Freed, I was recaptured a few days later, recognized on the boulevard by a captain with whom I'd had dealings for the October 31 affair. "So it's you, eh," he said, "the one who attacked Flourens for not having been energetic enough on October 31!" Four months later I escaped from the Chantier Prison in Versailles. Vermorel died around the same time as a result of his wounds, and even more of the ill treatment he suffered.

GEORGES PILOTELL

Director of the School Beaux-Arts and special commissar of the Commune

I send you my portrait of Maroteau, perhaps the sole anarchist of the Commune (and consequently the most slandered).

I am sorry that I can't send you the notes on the Commune you kindly request of me, but in the past month I haven't had a single moment to myself.

And then again, I admit that I would perhaps have been too severe toward our former friends. I'm not talking about those who were murdered, though death isn't an excuse, but of those narrow-minded sectarians with base desires, the mediocre ambitious men ready to content themselves with a bone thrown to them to nibble on: leaders, politicians, traitors.

Now there is something else that is emerging. In this nineteenth century of absolute authoritarianism magnificent anarchism is asserting itself philosophically and artistically.

I have only one hope, and it's that the Commune's errors will serve future demolishers.

M. LOUIS LUCIPIA
Municipal councilor of Paris

If the Republic didn't die in 1871 it's because the people of Paris didn't hesitate to rise up. This is my profound conviction, a conviction shared today by all those who, setting aside their personal social and political preferences, are willing to see the reality of facts.

M. CHAMPY
Member of the Commune, currently silversmith, worker representative on the labor relations board

We didn't only want to obtain municipal freedoms. If we had emerged victorious we would have organized the revolutionary movement throughout France. Victors, most of the large communes would have followed us, and the small follow the big.

But could you have emerged victorious?
I'm one of the only ones to have believed in victory. As for the twenty-two of the minority who, on May 15, declared they no longer wanted to sit on the pretext that the Commune, by creating the Committee of Public Safety, had created a dictatorship, this kind of defection weakened the Commune, but the force of events soon brought them back to the Commune. It wasn't the moment to throw out the baby with the bathwater. Another cause

of weakness was the abundance of Versaillais police informers and *agents provocateurs*, like Barral de Montaut, officer of the regular army who, presenting himself as a revolutionary, was named chief of the Seventh Legion. This Montaut was fertile in bizarre and bloody motions. After the Commune he was decorated with the Legion of Honor and named colonel.

Was the minority's claim to represent socialism justified?
No. There were excellent socialists in the majority, and more than the minority, the majority had a sense of the revolutionary situation. In truth, there was only a distinct minority for a few days.

In involving itself in affairs after the election of March 26, was the central Committee of the National Guard harmful?
The Central Committee wasn't as much of an encumbrance as has been said. It undoubtedly should have acted with more modesty when the Commune was elected. But in fact the division between the two powers was to an extent the work of Cluseret and Rossel; they always blamed the National Guard and the elected authorities for their errors.

Rossel?
Was obviously a good patriot in the strictest sense of the term. Once he was named delegate for war he appeared before us. As soon as he began speaking we all looked at each other and in a tacit and unanimous accord we restricted his mandate with the word "provisional." He dreamed of a dictatorship that would have allowed him to negotiate with Versailles while safeguarding, I would like to believe, Paris's rights. He wanted to have complete power, even civil. And so he attacked the Committee and the Commune when his military schemes failed. For me, even if I don't have any proof, when he was the chief of Cluseret's general staff he worked to supplant said Cluseret and intercepted certain orders that he was supposed to transmit to him. He never looked you in the eye.

Cluseret?
Cluseret constantly said "We have all the time in the world. No need to hurry." His inertia, his recurring negligence forced us to

remove his mandate as delegate for war and it was removed by a unanimous vote. We didn't see him again during the week of street fighting. In the end, Rossel was more serious.

Dombrowski?
How could he have let things reach a point there he could be suspected of treason? He was brought in by National Guardsmen at the moment, it is said, when he was going to go through the Prussian lines to flee the country. At the Hôtel de Ville he sobbed, "And to think that they believe I betrayed them." But no, he didn't betray. But he was disgusted to see the regular officers who made up his general staff betray him. He'd lost confidence. I was often at the front lines with him and he was never sparing of his life. In any case, as we all know, he was killed fighting. He had excellent troops. They weren't toy soldiers but men who were firmly resolute, hardened, brave, asking only to march. It's been too often said that the National Guard didn't form a serious army. Of the 240,000 men who composed it, the Commune had about a third at its disposal. Their number decreased daily, but there was still a large number of them at the end, and solid in the face of fire.

Do you believe there were traitors on the general staff?
Do you want to see them at work, these gentlemen of the general staff? I'll tell you about them. It's the Sunday morning when Ducatel handed over the Saint-Cloud gate and the Versaillais entered. If there was no one at the gate it was because the two battalions had been told that the troops that would be replacing them were only a couple of steps away. It wasn't customary for the defenders of the Commune to purely and simply abandon a post. As soon as I learned of Dombrowski's dispatch announcing the invasion of Paris I went to the war delegation with Gambon to find Delescluze. It was probably about 5:30. Delescluze shouted, "What is with you at the Commune? I sent officer after officer of the general staff to the front lines, but the enemy hasn't entered." "Are you certain of your officers?" "Yes, they've always seemed to be men I could count on. If one misled me, twenty couldn't." "I think that twenty did mislead you and I'm going there right now. Bring together the available National Guardsmen of the Seventh Legion."

Parizel,[19] one of the representatives of the seventh arrondissement, was given this charge. We arrived at the front lines and saw the Versaillais on our side of the gates. But with night falling they didn't dare advance; they were convinced that everything was going to blow up (they thought that Paris was mined) and were completely demoralized. Two prisoners brought to Delescluze told us this. I thought I'd find the Seventh Legion gathered, even if it was only a couple of thousand men. The plan would have been supported by artillery to launch them under cover of night like a wedge into the middle of the hesitating Versaillais mass; to, if need be, blow up a dozen caissons of artillery. And it is certain that, demoralized as they were, the invaders would have hastened to join the largest part of their troops, which were still behind the gates. But upon our return to the war delegation, at 8:30, there weren't even a hundred men who'd been gathered. Delescluze, half dead, was chewing on his eternal cigar butt. He looked at his officers. "What infamy! Betrayed by all!" and fell into his armchair, immediately bouncing back up. A gloomy silence. "Do like me and eat something." His dinner was served. Standing, we ate a piece of cold lamb. At daybreak the invasion began. We could no longer save either the Military School or the Champ de mars. On Monday [May] 22 the discouragement was immense. On the twenty-third Paris had gotten a grip on itself and the resistance seriously began. I thought victory was still possible. On the twenty-fifth we committed the error of allowing the Hôtel de Ville to be set on fire. On this subject many people have regretted allowing Pindy to remain there as governor.

Was this arson useful to the defense?
It was an enormous mistake that allowed Versailles to gain two days. The Hôtel de Ville and the fifth arrondissement, connected to the thirteenth arrondissement and some of the southern forts, constituted an almost impregnable line of fortifications. The Versaillais weren't advancing. Because of the fires we lost the fourth and fifth arrondissements with the Pantheon, the

---

19. Francois Parizel (1841–1877)—Physician. Member of the Commune, representing the seventeenth arrondissement. Exiled to the U.S., where he was active in the socialist movement, dying in Newark, New Jersey.

thirteenth and the entire line of southern forts (Montrouge, Vanves, Moulin-Sacquet, and Hautes-Bruyères) with 120 cannons and ten thousand *fédérés* who were used to fighting. Then there was the retreat to the eleventh arrondissement, the concentration of the resistance on Belleville, the invasion of the twentieth arrondissement, and finally on Monday morning, the twenty-ninth, the surrender of the fort at Vincennes. I have to insist that the defenders of the Commune, leaders and soldiers, in general did their duty both outside the walls and on the streets. I consider this to have been not a riot or an insurrection, but a revolution, and it saved the Republic.

Don't you think that the Commune was too timorous in financial matters, in particular as regards the Bank of France?
We were so busy! We didn't give the issue enough importance. We occupied the Bank, but in truth we didn't make use of the way today's revolutionary party would. But our intention was to set an economic example for everyone, to show that the working people could govern themselves economically. The National Guard received thirty sous daily, but food supplies were never lacking behind the barricades. And if the pay had been higher, we wouldn't have had any more combatants. If we had wasted even a little bit, we would have been going against popular sentiment. Nevertheless, I recognize that we could have used the Bank in order to attempt to get M. Thiers to settle with us. And Jourde didn't make the facts clear to us the way he should have. Had he done so there is no doubt but that we would have removed all obstacles. Jourde was lacking in temperament.

M. CHAUVIÈRE
Currently deputy

1. A member of the Central Committee of the National Guard, I resigned at the moment of the elections to the Commune, where the fourteenth arrondissement gave me a thousand votes (I wasn't elected—I was nineteen). I was secretary to General Duval at the prefecture of police, which I left to go to the Chatillon plateau where, on April 4, I was taken prisoner along with 1,600 others, including Elisée Reclus, Trousset, Colonel Henri, etc. I saw Duval executed, and his friends Maugé and Lecoeur of the 103rd Battalion (fifteenth arrondissement) who died gallantly. From there it was the Golgotha of Versailles, under jeers and blows, transport to Quélern, return to Versailles, to Rambouillet; court-martial at Rambouillet, sentenced to five years in prison and as many years under surveillance.

2. Parliamentary organization: a detestable minority busier with legislating than with organizing the defense and taking bold measures, hindering the action of those who were vigorous. Lack of cohesion as a result of the absence of the direction needed in a battle in which Paris fought alone against France and the rest.

Military organization: poor, though they had everything needed to win in just a few days. Too much slowness, too much hesitation, a deplorable optimism, calling retreats victories; no unity.

Financial organization: admirable, if they'd used the financial might contained in the Bank they would perhaps have saved the military situation. This touched the bourgeois soul.

Administrative organization: excellent, as everyone admits.

3. The influence: Enormous. The proletariat that burst on the scene in June 1848 was crushed and surrendered in the face of slander. June seemed to be a combat against the parliamentarians of the reactionary National Assembly, but with this going against it, that it appeared at the same time that it was against the Republic.

They cast a new light on June. The Commune, a kind of jacquerie, was at first patriotic, prepared by the events of the siege and helped along by the cowardice of the Government of National Defense. It became a popular government rebelling against the other government. It was a bold act of internationalism in the face of the invasion it would have combated had it defeated Versailles. It placed the social problem, a problem until then was locked away in little-read or forgotten books, before the people. It was a lesson for the future. The unforeseen event that it was can always be renewed. Six months before no one who would have predicted it would have been believed. It demonstrated what we could do and also that the oligarchies can't resist a violent, rapid, persistent attack of conscious democracies inspired by minorities devoted unto the ultimate sacrifice.

A black mark. The horrible executions certainly diminished Parisian energy. They struck everything that had an open and courageous appearance. The daring, on the other hand, who were able to escape the wall and the soldier-judges took refuge overseas. They expanded socialism's sphere of influence, but the necessary point of action was deserted, and long days are needed to reconstitute it. One has to have known some of those who are dead in order to judge the loss suffered: Flourens, Duval, Ferré, Rigault, etc., to speak only of those I knew. It will return and is returning, but it has tarried for a long time.

ALEXANDER THOMPSON

Currently editor of The Clarion *of London. He was eight at the time of the Commune*

I lived with my parents on the Boulevard Saint-Michel across from the Luxembourg Gardens. On both sides of the house there were barricades constructed under the direction of a lovely Amazon whose beauty, charming manners, and ever-ready revolver led every passerby to lend assistance.

Our barricades, I can call them this because everyone in the house worked on them, were ready on the twenty-third, but the tide didn't reach us until the twenty-fourth. The previous night the cannonade had been continuous and the resistance was carried out furiously in the Luxembourg Gardens. Suddenly, a horrible explosion smashed everything in the house and broke all the windows. It was the powder magazine of the Luxembourg that the retreating Communards had blown up.

It was now the turn of the barricade that closed off the Rue Soufflot. Two women, probably his mother and sister, were trying to drag away a beardless Communard, but the Amazon shouted at them, "Get lost," and the two women found themselves between the barricade and the gate of the garden when the firing began.

A young Versaillais officer ran into the street, a white handkerchief in his hand, and though the firing continued he succeeded in dragging the two women to the shelter of the trees of the promenade.

During the combat we took refuge in the cellar, listening, in the intervals between the crackling of the machine guns and the cannon fire, to the lamentations of a tenant of the house. He predicted that if we weren't killed by the balls we would be buried alive, for they were supposed to blow up the Pantheon during their retreat and the roof of the building would collapse on our house.

The discussion was interrupted by a frantic young Communard who shouted that the barricade was taken and begged us to hide him. We found a ladder and helped him to jump over the courtyard wall, but a Versaillais aimed at him from a window and killed him.

There then arrived an enraged Versaillais captain who threw himself of the frightened troop of women and children, crying that if one sole Communard was found in the house everyone would be executed.

While going back upstairs we found two Communards killed on the flagstones of the vestibule. Upstairs, in my room, a blood covered soldier stretched out on the bed. In the street a Communard was laid out flat, brought down by the Versaillais balls.

On the barricade on the Rue Soufflot, rifle in hand, we saw the Amazon laid out. In mockery a Versaillais opened her clothing with the point of his saber, and the soldiers laughed at this.

J. MARTELET
Member of the Commune

I have always thought that the communalist movement of 1871 had to advance, knowing from the experience of the siege how dangerous it was to be cautious. We knew that what we were leaving behind was bad and that it wasn't difficult to do better. The majority of the new representatives from Paris were resolved to definitively proclaim the rights of the majority of the nation, that is, the workers. The Commune proved this by voting the first three economic decrees that it was essential to immediately take care of: rents, debts, and the National Guard. These decrees nevertheless frightened the Versailles government, which saw that the program we affirmed was something different from the usual political programs.

There was a majority and a minority in the Commune. The men of the majority, of which I was one, wanted to have done with Versailles as soon as possible, and mostly proposed combat measures. The minority was more preoccupied with economic questions. It was convinced that reminiscences of the politics of yesteryear would do the social revolution no good and it refused to vote for the Committee of Public Safety.

We found ourselves side by side during the terrible Bloody Week, majority and minority, fighting with the same ardor until the final day of the fight, defending together with the same faith the rights of the working people.

MADAME N.

My husband was the commander of the Twenty-Second Battalion of the National Guard. I was very young at the time and was living on the Île Saint-Louis. I was only vaguely aware of what was going on in Paris. Our island was relatively calm. The Versaillais had isolated it. The Wednesday or Thursday of the final week I heard some brouhaha and on the staircase an irritated voice said, "There's a commander in the house." I was in the process of making coffee. I opened the door, my filter in my hand. Some chasseurs from Vincennes were there, rifles at the ready, commanded by a young officer with a self-important air. I didn't at all realize the danger. This deployment of forces and the swaggering air of the little officer, all of this made me laugh, which annoyed him. "Your husband?" "He's not here." "He acted like the cowards and fled." "I'm sure you understand that he wasn't going to wait for you here." They searched all the furniture and they scattered around the packets of letters. The little officer, straightening himself up, said with nobility, "I'm a member of the Randon family, madame." (The Randons were big wine merchants on the Île Saint-Louis.) I answered, "They're the ones who sold me my wine." Then he said, "I regret, Madame, that they sold to canaille like you at the same time that they serve honorable men, men who provision the army." I found the young officer ridiculous and wasn't yet frightened. But then they made me leave. First they took me to Notre Dame, then to the Place du Châtelet. There was firing on the right and the left. I saw a young man with beautiful black hair that I was told was Vallès. He fell, crying, "Vive la République!" As soon as we crossed the bridges I was insulted, mostly by women.

By elegant women?

By women of the people. I saw one in a red camisole and worn-out shoes, standing on a bench and shouting, "Oh, that damn whore! She has new bottines and we don't even have shoes." If I wasn't torn to pieces at the beginning of my voyage I probably owe it to the modest air I then had, the air of a little church-goer, with a waterproof and a black hat. My soldiers had a hard time controlling the crowd, though. They shouted, "Spank her! Take away her chignon!" We were now on the way to the Place Vendôme. I saw houses burning, smoking, helmeted firemen. It looked like a theater set. As I walked people shouted at me that I was a *pétroleuse*. All was calm on the Place Vendôme. Filthy soldiers, black with powder, were resting. They were being brought a young *pétroleuse*. I learned that this was one of the soldiers' jokes. Without stopping at the Place Vendôme I was sent on to the Châtelet. What they were looking for, I think, was what in military language is called the stronghold.

I didn't have the heart to go down the Rue de Rivoli again. I had been too insulted there. My soldiers agreed to go via the Rue Saint-Honoré. I'm still grateful to them. Now we were at the Châtelet. I was led to the foyer. It was full of people in the most desperate poses. I thought of the famous painting "The Appeal of the Condemned" [Mme N. is the wife of a painter], which made me smile. But I was immediately in despair, for the soldiers who had arrested me, who consequently knew something about me and who I considered my safeguard, were leaving. First they registered Mme Régère. She had on her the sash that belonged to her husband, a member of the Commune. She was in half mourning and had white flowers on her hat, which gave rise to many military puns. And yet she was quite modest, as well. In order to insult us you really had to want to. That day we didn't eat anything.

The next day?
The next day at about 11:00 we were made to go down to the stronghold. We were made to link arms in groups of seven and we left, escorted by chasseurs from Versailles. The lieutenant who commanded the convoy seemed to be ashamed. He didn't dare look at us even once. I only saw women, since I was walking in the front, but it appears there were men in the rear. We were going to Satory. It was raining. We were filthy. Many were wearing old, broken-down shoes. Along the way a woman asked for stockings when she passed by a millinery store. The merchant distributed stockings and we paid if we wanted to. He was nearly arrested. One of us was dressed in brown silk. She was spattered with mud. When you're holding someone's arm you can't lift your dress. A very ugly woman had a crinoline, though this was no longer the fashion. The soldiers spoke of nothing but giving us saber blows if we gave any sign of stopping. We halted in a forest and our infantrymen were replaced by cavalrymen. The new officer looked at us mockingly. With the point of his saber he tore my and Mme Régère's veils. Having not eaten since the previous day our throats were parched from having walked since the morning. The officers were much crueler than the soldiers.

We had started off again and now we had to march as quickly as the horses. We arrived at Satory during the night. There we were parked in a room that was already packed with people. These poor women prisoners made a poor impression. There was a litter of straw on the ground that the humidity soon caused to ferment. Days passed. We swarmed about sounding like crawfish in a stench of blood, urine and sweat, amid the fleas, bedbugs, and cockroaches. We were all suffering from colic. The doctor could only give us a little bit of laudanum. One bread per day, nothing else, and dirty water in a can, but very little, barely what we needed to drink. During the night all our legs were all tangled together, to such an extent that it was impossible to sleep. A gendarme procured food for us and stole from us. After an absence of a few days he reappeared. In the interim he'd been decorated.

The time passed. All these women were without linen. All who were pregnant had had miscarriages. Can you imagine all this, women having miscarriages guarded by soldiers? We hardly spoke to each other.

Behind our billet there was a small field. In order to go there you had to ask permission. But there were always officers observing. I spent seventeen days without going to the toilet. They transferred me to Versailles. Things were much better there. Everyone had his own bundle of straw. We made mattresses. During the day we piled the mattresses one on top of another to have sofas. Louise Michel and I wrote letters for the other women. All these women would have done anything in the world to have Louise Michel's approval. They distributed wood to us, but uncut; rice, but we didn't have salt, butter, or a pot. Telling us to eat was a form of irony. Little by little vegetable sellers were able to set up a kind of kitchen.

Above us there were 150 kids, almost all of them paperboys. During the night they shouted the titles of the revolutionary newspapers, to the great indignation of the guards. These kids were now in rags. When their backsides were too obvious there was a distribution of old breeches of gendarmes. Little Ranvier, twelve years old, son of a member of the Commune, refused this military garb.

Louise Michel had been transferred to another prison, Avenue de Versailles, no. 20. I had remained in the Chantier Prison near the train station. We wrote to each other to tell about what was happening to each of us, letters that were naturally subject to administrative censorship.

Did you keep these letters?
Here are a few, but they're of no interest.

(We reproduce the letters below, considering them to be characteristic.)

> July 7
> My good friend;
>
> I find myself embarrassed. Mme Montet is ill and we promised her daughter to look after her, so I have to tell her. But do it in such a way that she doesn't think the illness worse than it is: it's the sorrow of separation.
>
> If someone or some package arrives for me send it here, and at the same time send me a bottle, a small one, the liter is broken.
>
> Tell me how you are and don't allow boredom to defeat you. Did you write to mama? Above all tell her everything that could console her.
>
> Did Mme David finally receive her package?
>
> Do you write all the letters for the ladies and do you give paper for these of the children?
>
> I am quite annoyed at the thought that you have remained without any money. Tell me if your mother has returned?
>
> Embrace all our friends for me and tell those who think of me how much I hope for the end of their problems.
>
> My love to Marie Drée, to those ladies who came to us. I shake everyone's hand.
>
> Louise Michel
>
> Try to see to it that they don't forget the madwoman

> July 27, 1871
> Dear friend,
>
> Why don't you answer? Are you still at the station? We can't know because the woman who just arrived here doesn't

know who has left or who has arrived since our departure. Tell us this.

Why don't you ask to come to us? We work, which helps the long days pass.

We embrace and love you.

I knew that Félicie Glingamer was free. Is poor Hortense free too? Tell me also if Marie Drée has left. Anyway, I see that you've forgotten both of us since it takes you so long to answer. As for us, we forget no one. Tell Mme Neel that now with her glasses she can write.

Don't forget to send our regards to our friends and a warm handshake for all.

We embrace you.

Louise Michel
20 Rue de Paris

Has Mme Dijon forgotten me? Is Mme David still there? All those ladies who like to be busy would be less bored here. Mme Guguema received a letter from her husband. I haven't forgotten Victorine or Justine or anyone.

My dearest friend,

Your letter finally reached us. As for the details of our lives, the only ones are that we think of you often, that the sisters are very polite, and that working at jewelry-making distracts us. As for news of you, we need to hear everything. First, I embrace everyone, even the wicked ones. It goes without saying that I doubly embrace my friends. Poor grumbler, you must be bored. That lately Mmes. Nesle, Marie Drée, Jeanne the medical assistant, David, and so many others that I seem to see around me and whose names escape me, that's how rapidly and dreamlike we live at the current time.

I send you all my heart. Especially when we're separated we feel how strong prison friendships are.

Write us as soon as you can. Send us news of everyone, don't forget the woman with the pious stories or Félicie Glingamer, Mme Comte or any of the new ones who know me by chance. Don't forget fat Lucy if she doesn't tease the others and Victorine.

I embrace you on behalf of everyone.

Louise Michel

Félicie wrote to Mme Ménier but she didn't receive an answer. Do you write these ladies' letters? Do you give the kids paper? Do you write their letters? Do they give the madwoman something to eat?

Were you brutalized?
Here's one story among many. Near the fountain a corporal was kicking a young man in the belly who had arrived from Evreux with his mother. He was guilty of having answered the women who spoke to him. The latter having issued "ahhhs" of reprobation: "If you don't shut up you'll receive the same," and immediately he struck out at them with some rope. At precisely that moment I passed, holding a can of sardines in my hand.

The ablutions of the Commune?
Instinctively I struck the brigadier on the back with the can. He threw himself on me and beat me until I fainted. My shoes had fallen off and I was carried out barefoot. There were shouts from the women in the prison and a crowd gathered in the street. The lieutenant arrived, furious: "You have the nerve to yell at us. Know that we have the right of life or death over you." The women who'd been beaten were attached to pillars, their hands behind their backs. It makes you sick to the stomach to have your hands behind your back, you have no idea! A little bit later we were taken to a riding school. Sailors attached us, our hands still behind our backs, to a tree. During the night we managed to untie ourselves. We passed the time singing "Le Chant du Départ" that one of us, Mme Dijon, a really funny woman, had on her cuffs. Suddenly there was a light under the door. It was midnight and we put our hands back in the ropes. A corporal entered; he wasn't fooled and he reattached us. He addressed himself to me, "You're the damn whore who beat me." I didn't answer, closing my eyes as I waited to be slapped. The next day there was a visit from Superintendent Clément. The scandal was known in the

city. Clément made a big speech to us. He told us that during the great revolution this happened and that happened but that what caused the revolution was envy. He wouldn't stop. Most didn't know what he was talking about. He threatened us with Saint-Lazare and finally was willing to pardon us. He was excessively solemn and all the more laughable. He was perched on the staircase to harangue us. He was huffing and puffing like mad.

During our detention the man we had the most to complaint about was a lieutenant named Marcerou. This guy, for anything at all, whipped people's faces and kicked them. Many women were ill, some went mad. There were women who had children at home. I was among the first freed. It was in the month of August 1871.

GENERAL DE GALLIFET

Sir:

It is impossible for me to answer the questions you do me the honor of posing.

Please accept my most humble respects,

General Gallifet

■ ABOUT MITCHELL ABIDOR

Mitchell Abidor is the principal French translator for the Marxists Internet Archive and has published several collections of his translations, including *Anarchists Never Surrender: Essays, Polemics, and Correspondence on Anarchism* by Victor Serge. He is currently working on translations of further unpublished works by Victor Serge and Daniel Guérin.

ABOUT PM PRESS

PM Press was founded at the end of 2007 by a small collection of folks with decades of publishing, media, and organizing experience. PM Press co-conspirators have published and distributed hundreds of books, pamphlets, CDs, and DVDs. Members of PM have founded enduring book fairs, spearheaded victorious tenant organizing campaigns, and worked closely with bookstores, academic conferences, and even rock bands to deliver political and challenging ideas to all walks of life. We're old enough to know what we're doing and young enough to know what's at stake.

We seek to create radical and stimulating fiction and non-fiction books, pamphlets, T-shirts, visual and audio materials to entertain, educate, and inspire you. We aim to distribute these through every available channel with every available technology—whether that means you are seeing anarchist classics at our bookfair stalls; reading our latest vegan cookbook at the café; downloading geeky fiction e-books; or digging new music and timely videos from our website.

PM Press is always on the lookout for talented and skilled volunteers, artists, activists, and writers to work with. If you have a great idea for a project or can contribute in some way, please get in touch.

PM Press
PO Box 23912
Oakland, CA 94623
www.pmpress.org

FRIENDS OF PM PRESS

These are indisputably momentous times—
the financial system is melting down globally
and the Empire is stumbling. Now more than
ever there is a vital need for radical ideas.

In the seven years since its founding—and on a mere shoestring—
PM Press has risen to the formidable challenge of publishing and
distributing knowledge and entertainment for the struggles ahead.
With over 300 releases to date, we have published an impressive
and stimulating array of literature, art, music, politics, and culture.
Using every available medium, we've succeeded in connecting those
hungry for ideas and information to those putting them into practice.

Friends of PM allows you to directly help impact, amplify, and
revitalize the discourse and actions of radical writers, filmmakers, and
artists. It provides us with a stable foundation from which we can
build upon our early successes and provides a much-needed subsidy
for the materials that can't necessarily pay their own way. You can
help make that happen—and receive every new title automatically
delivered to your door once a month—by joining as a Friend of PM
Press. And, we'll throw in a free T-shirt when you sign up.

Here are your options (all include a 50% discount on all webstore
purchases):
* **$30 a month** Get all books and pamphlets
* **$40 a month** Get all PM Press releases (including CDs and DVDs)
* **$100 a month** Everything plus PM merchandise and free downloads

For those who can't afford $30 or more a month, we're introducing
Sustainer Rates at $15, $10 and $5. Sustainers get a free PM Press
T-shirt and a 50% discount on all purchases from our website.

Your Visa or Mastercard will be billed once a month, until you tell
us to stop. Or until our efforts succeed in bringing the revolution
around. Or the financial meltdown of Capital makes plastic
redundant. Whichever comes first.

Anarchists Never Surrender: Essays, Polemics, and Correspondence on Anarchism, 1908–1938

Victor Serge • Editor: Mitchell Abidor • Foreword: Richard Greeman

ISBN: 978-1-62963-031-1
$20.00 • 256 Pages

Anarchists Never Surrender provides a complete picture of Victor Serge's relationship to anarchism. The volume contains writings going back to his teenage years in Brussels, where he became influenced by the doctrine of individualist anarchism. At the heart of the anthology are key articles written soon after his arrival in Paris in 1909, when he became editor of the newspaper *l'anarchie*. In these articles Serge develops and debates his own radical thoughts, arguing the futility of mass action and embracing "illegalism." Serge's involvement with the notorious French group of anarchist armed robbers, the Bonnot Gang, landed him in prison for the first time in 1912. *Anarchists Never Surrender* includes both his prison correspondence with his anarchist comrade Émile Armand and articles written immediately after his release.

The book also includes several articles and letters written by Serge after he had left anarchism behind and joined the Russian Bolsheviks in 1919. Here Serge analyzed anarchism and the ways in which he hoped anarchism would leaven the harshness and dictatorial tendencies of Bolshevism. Included here are writings on anarchist theory and history, Bakunin, the Spanish revolution, and the Kronstadt uprising.

Anarchists Never Surrender anthologizes Victor Serge's previously unavailable texts on anarchism and fleshes out the portrait of this brilliant writer and thinker, a man I.F. Stone called one of the "moral figures of our time."

> "One of the most compelling of twentieth-century ethical and literary heroes."
> —Susan Sontag

Outrage:
An Anarchist Memoir of the
Penal Colony

Clément Duval
Translator: Michael Shreve
Introduction: Marianne Enckell
ISBN: 978-1-60486-500-4
$20.00 • 224 Pages

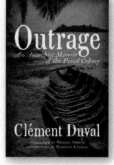

"Theft exists only through the exploitation of man by man...when Society refuses you the right to exist, you must take it...the policeman arrested me in the name of the Law, I struck him in the name of Liberty."

In 1887, Clément Duval joined the tens of thousands of convicts sent to the "dry guillotine" of the French penal colonies. Few survived and fewer were able to tell the stories of their life in that hell. Duval spent fourteen years doing hard labor—espousing the values of anarchism and demonstrating the ideals by being a living example the entire time—before making his daring escape and arriving in New York City, welcomed by the Italian and French anarchists there.

This is much more than an historical document about the anarchist movement and the penal colony. It is a remarkable story of survival by one man's self-determination, energy, courage, loyalty, and hope. It was thanks to being true and faithful to his ideals that Duval survived life in this hell. Unlike the well-known prisoner Papillon, who arrived and dramatically escaped soon after Duval, he encouraged his fellow prisoners to practice mutual aid, through their deeds and not just their words. It is a call to action for mindful, conscious people to fight for their rights to the very end, to never give up or give in.

More than just a story of a life or a testament of ideals, here is a monument to the human spirit and a war cry for freedom and justice.

Anarchy, Geography, Modernity: Selected Writings of Elisée Reclus

Elisée Reclus
Editors: John P. Clark and
Camille Martin
ISBN: 978-1-60486-429-8
$22.95 • 304 Pages

Anarchy, Geography, Modernity is the first comprehensive introduction to the thought of Elisée Reclus, the great anarchist geographer and political theorist. It shows him to be an extraordinary figure for his age. Not only an anarchist but also a radical feminist, anti-racist, ecologist, animal rights advocate, cultural radical, nudist, and vegetarian. Not only a major social thinker but also a dedicated revolutionary.

The work analyzes Reclus' greatest achievement, a sweeping historical and theoretical synthesis recounting the story of the earth and humanity as an epochal struggle between freedom and domination. It presents his groundbreaking critique of all forms of domination: not only capitalism, the state, and authoritarian religion, but also patriarchy, racism, technological domination, and the domination of nature. His crucial insights on the interrelation between personal and small-group transformation, broader cultural change, and large-scale social organization are explored. Reclus' ideas are presented both through detailed exposition and analysis, and in extensive translations of key texts, most appearing in English for the first time.

> "Maintaining an appropriately scholarly style, marked by deep background knowledge, nuanced argument, and careful qualifications, Clark and Martin nevertheless reveal a passionate love for their subject and adopt a stance of political engagement that they hope does justice to Reclus' own commitments."
> —*Historical Geography*